T0279883

SOUL MATES OF THE LOST GENERATION

Soul Mates of the Lost Generation

The Letters of John Dos Passos and Crystal Ross

Lewis M. Dabney

UNIVERSITY OF VIRGINIA PRESS

Charlottesville and London

University of Virginia Press
© 2022 by the Estate of Lewis M. Dabney III
All rights reserved
Printed in the United States of America on acid-free paper

First published 2022

ISBN 978-0-8139-4867-6 (hardcover)
ISBN 978-0-8139-4868-3 (ebook)

1 3 5 7 9 8 6 4 2

Library of Congress Cataloging-in-Publication Data
is available for this title.

Cover art: Crystal Ross Dabney (courtesy of Elizabeth Hochman and the family
of Lewis Dabney) and John Dos Passos (John Dos Passos Papers, 1865–1999,
Accession #5950, Box 133, Special Collections, University of Virginia Library)

CONTENTS

FOREWORD

In 1924, the year that a young Texan by the name of Crystal Ross spent wonderful weeks in Europe with the novelist John Dos Passos, another novelist, Virginia Woolf, described a dramatic shift in human experience. "On or about December 1910," Woolf observed in a lecture that was published as "Mr. Bennett and Mrs. Brown," "human character changed." Crystal Ross, the protagonist of the remarkable book that Lewis Dabney, the older of her two sons, has crafted from the letters that she and Dos Passos exchanged, flourished in that changing world. "All human relations have shifted," Woolf declared, "—those between masters and servants, husbands and wives, parents and children. And when human relations change there is at the same time a change in religion, conduct, politics, and literature." Crystal was born in 1900. Her father was a respected small-town Texas doctor. In her twenties she lived on her own in Austin, Texas, and in Europe, completed work on a *doctorat* at the University of Strasbourg, and fell in love with a promising but impecunious young writer. Crystal and Dos, as he was known, first met in New York. Their romance grew in France and Spain.

Soul Mates of the Lost Generation is a story of the Jazz Age. In the correspondence that documents Crystal's evolving relationship with Dos we witness the changes in human character that fascinated Woolf. Crystal had a physical ease and a fearlessness that many young women were coming in those years to regard as their birthright. She was an excellent swimmer, enjoyed being behind the wheel of a car, thought nothing of traveling by herself, and loved to dance at a time when the Charleston was at the height of its popularity. She embraced the playfulness but also the seriousness of the 1920s. She leapt at the possibility of a woman's pursuing intellectual and professional goals that had in earlier times been options only for men. She never really doubted that she had what it took to obtain an advanced academic degree or teach in a college and was thrilled by the spirit of experimentation in the arts that she saw at first hand through her affair with Dos. Crystal got to know his great friend Ernest Hemingway and apparently even read the proofs of Hemingway's collection of stories *In Our Time* before it was published by Boni and Liveright in 1925. She visited Gertrude Stein and Alice B. Toklas in Paris, where the walls of their apartment were lined with Picasso's paintings. She spent an evening in Montmartre with Zelda Fitzgerald and was introduced to Ezra Pound at a café. Dos Passos hoped that while she was in Paris she would see *Les noces,* the ballet with music by Stravinsky and choreography by a woman, Bronislava Nijinska, that brought new qualities of sight and sound to the stage.

This young woman from Texas was present at the creation of what amounted to a revolution in American fiction, characterized by language that was sharp, clear, and austere and themes that shattered the old narrative conventions in favor of striking juxtapositions and ambiguous conclusions. Dos Passos was in the thick of writing *Manhattan Transfer,* the collage of a novel that he devoted to the shifting fortunes of New Yorkers and the forever-changing rhythms of the city. In 1926 Hemingway published *The Sun Also Rises,* which opens with Gertrude Stein's famous declaration: "You are all a lost generation."

Crystal, who was with Dos Passos and Hemingway in Pamplona in 1924, is referred to in the book's early pages as "a girl in Strasbourg who can show us the town." She was an indomitable spirit. But she was also a member of that enigmatic cohort that Stein had dubbed "a lost generation." Having seen firsthand the world immortalized in *The Sun Also Rises*, she must have known both the exhilarating embrace of pure experience that Hemingway described in his limpid prose and the underlying uncertainty that he suggested through his unwillingness to give the novel some grand, overarching design. The novels that Dos Passos and Hemingway were working on in the mid-1920s, when Crystal and Dos were romantically involved, are at least in part about the limits of freedom.

As much as *Soul Mates of the Lost Generation* is a love story, it's also an exploration of the promises and perils of modernity. Although Crystal enjoyed uprooting old conventions and overturning old habits, she remained attentive to the expectations of her family and the world in which she had been born. Her eager embrace of an independent life—as student, teacher, and lover, both in the United States and Europe—was followed by a return to what cannot but seem a more conventional path for a woman of her time and place. According to her son, she set aside her own intellectual and professional ambitions as she turned to the duties of a wife and a mother. Her wit, energy, and intelligence remained, now as accompaniments to her husband's distinguished career as a lawyer in Washington and New York. Her son's enthusiastic description of a couple of brilliant essays about Hemingway that Crystal wrote for the *Dallas News* in 1927 lends poignancy to the abrupt end of her young career. But Crystal's life was anything but tragic. Although her son credits himself only with editing these letters, what he's actually done is shape them into a remarkable tale. A lost life has been found. Whatever the limitations of the life that Crystal ultimately chose to live—and every life has its limits and hers was in many respects a fulfilling one—she endures in these pages as big, brave, and beguiling.

There is no mystery as to why Lewis Dabney assembled *Soul Mates of the Lost Generation* in the last years of his life. (He was eighty-three when he died in 2015.) It was an act of filial piety—a celebration of the mother whom he loved. But there was another, perhaps equally personal impulse. This book forms a sort of coda to Dabney's life work, the definitive biography of Edmund Wilson that he published in 2005. There had been a time when John Dos Passos and Edmund Wilson were good friends. By saluting his mother's connection with Dos—they seem to have remained in touch throughout their lives—Dabney was closing the circle, demonstrating his own connection with Dos Passos and thus with Wilson. Dabney says as much in the preface to his biography, where he recalls that when he first met Wilson they discussed "Dos Passos and Hemingway, my mother's friends in France during the twenties, whom I had met as a boy." Dabney had received an invitation to visit Wilson after publishing a review of Wilson's *Patriotic Gore* in the *Columbia University Forum* in 1962. Writing about this monumental study of the literature of the Civil War, he praised Wilson's ability "to show qualities of character, temperament, and style as these develop in each subject's story and work." Among the revelations of *Patriotic Gore,* as Dabney described them, are Wilson's ability to demonstrate how "the diaries of Southern ladies could be works of art." I wouldn't be surprised if Dabney was thinking about Wilson's genius for discovering wonderful literature in unexpected places as he transformed the letters that his mother and Dos had exchanged into a work of considerable literary value. For Dabney, as for many men and women who came of age in the 1940s and 1950s, the 1920s were a fascinating mirage, a time of hope all too soon shattered by an onslaught of horrors: the Depression, World War II, the Holocaust, the Blitz, Hiroshima, the Gulags. In *Soul Mates of the Lost Generation* Crystal Ross stands before us, strong in body and spirit, an embodiment of the modern age.

Jed Perl

PREFACE

As a son of one of the principals in the story these unpublished letters tell, I owe the reader an account of how I came to edit them and of my sources insofar as they are not in the public record. Growing up, I knew that my mother, Crystal Ross Dabney, took her *doctorat* at the University of Strasbourg in France in 1923–25 and was engaged to John Dos Passos before marrying my father in 1927. She had met Dos, as she called him (pronounced "Doss" not "Dose"), in New York and corresponded with him from the University of Texas in Austin and her home in the nearby small town of Lockhart. They fell in love in Paris and Spain, their relationship one of the "secrets" alluded to in the preface to the memoir *A Moveable Feast,* where Hemingway contrasts them to stories "everybody knows." Crystal's *doctorat* was in comparative literature, her dissertation comparing O. Henry and Guy de Maupassant written in French and defended in French before "six men in red robes and purple hats." She and Dos were engaged while she wrote the dissertation in Strasbourg, and in Brooklyn Heights Dos wrote *Manhattan Transfer* (1925), one of the best novels of New York in the twenties. Though Crystal was let down by the long thesis struggle, the two reviews of Hemingway's early fiction she afterward completed for the *Dallas News* mark a critical gift that would have been better known had she not married Lewis Dabney before disappearing in the shadows of literary history.

In my youth she said little of Dos, yet the lengthening row of his books on our shelves made a conspicuous presence with which my father seemed comfortable. Dos Passos and Hemingway were close friends then, and when my brother and I read modern literature in college, Mother told us she had seen a good deal of Hemingway and Hadley, had sat at the feet of Gertrude Stein. Dos and she were at Pamplona in the summer of 1924. She was reassuringly unlike Lady Duff Twysden, the Brett Ashley character in the next summer's group, the cast of *The Sun Also Rises*. But Hemingway sets Crystal Ross in their generation's roster as that novel begins. At a table in Paris with Frances Clyne, Jake Barnes suggests to his restless friend Cohn that they go up to Strasbourg, where "a swell girl" can show them the town. She has been there two years, he says, and knows everything about that small city in Alsace-Lorraine, German after 1870, returned to France by the Treaty of Versailles.

I met Dos Passos when starting my own Ph.D. in 1957, driving Mother and him to a meeting of the American Academy of Arts and Letters where William Faulkner presented his colleague the Gold Medal for fiction. That was the evening when, after too much wine and speeches too long for his taste, Faulkner put aside his text and, handing the medal to Dos, declared, "Nobody deserved it more or had to wait for it longer." Dos Passos's gentlemanly manners were not what I expected of a rebellious radical, but we commiserated over the Bates Method of eye exercise, to which Mother had subjected me during my teens. Dos was loyal to its regimen although his first wife, Katy, the older sister of Hem's friend Bill Smith, had been killed in 1947 in an auto accident the Bates Method helped bring on. Dos Passos and Mother met several times in their later years, and I drove her to the novelist's memorial service in 1970.

While working in the University of Virginia Library in 1971, I had the early letters between them copied. They take Crystal from Lockhart, Texas, in 1923 through the completion of her Ph.D. at Strasbourg in May 1925. In a bureau drawer, she had other letters she told me should be in the same collection, some from the later years of their lives. My mother's memories stand behind her letters and are the primary source of the tale that follows. The couple became close friends only eight years after the death of Dos's mother, Lucy Addison Sprigg Madison, a Virginian twenty-four years widowed when her son was born in 1896, and five years after the death of Lucy's lover and Dos's father, a Portuguese immigrant's son. A New York criminal attorney who became a top corporation lawyer, John Randolph Dos Passos didn't marry Lucy or make their relationship public until the death of his Catholic wife in 1910. Called Jack Madison until he took his father's name in 1912, the future novelist had two older half brothers: his mother's son, named James Madison for the president (her ancestor), and his father's son, Louis Hays Dos Passos.

There were boyhood summers on the 8,000-plus acres of Virginia farmland his father—in the novelist's memoirs "the Commodore"—purchased along the Potomac and traveled to by steam yacht from Washington, as Dos explains in the brilliant early chapters of *The Best Times* (1966). Dos's first language was French, and three years at Choate weren't easy for a nonathletic literary boy whose English could sound like a foreigner's. At Harvard he came into his own among like-minded friends, reading more, writing more than the others, who recalled him as energetic and convivial. But Lucy's situation had worn her down, and she died in the spring of 1915, Dos's junior year. He and his father spent less time together after his mother's death, but their correspondence swelled, though it was only in Dos's later years that he recognized the mark his father's culture and political values had made. The Commodore sent him with a tutor on a six-month grand tour after he passed his Harvard entrance exams, helped pay for the printing of his first book, and was supporting Dos as an art student in

Spain when he suddenly died of galloping pneumonia in January 1917. He had made and spent a large fortune, and the gangling youth who spoke and dressed as a gentleman, but whose arms, legs, and neck were altogether too long, inherited the Virginia estate with his half brother Louis. Dos wanted little to do with money or property, living on literature and on pittances doled out by his mother's sister—the Aunt Protectoress, as he naively put it—until he had to sue them for a small fortune during his forties.

Dos Passos's fiction is at its best when autobiographical. His service with the Norton-Harjes Ambulance Service during World War I led to the once famous antiwar novel *Three Soldiers.* Through the Jazz Age and the Depression he welded a reporter's appetite for facts to modernist experiment. Hugo Bamman as a stand-in for the young Dos in Edmund Wilson's *I Thought of Daisy* (1929) turns out solidly built books to purge the weaknesses of the cultivated bourgeoisie from whom he comes, whom he thinks compromised by capitalism. The author of *Manhattan Transfer* (1925) and the trilogy *U.S.A.* (*The 42nd Parallel* [1932], *Nineteen Nineteen* [1934], *The Big Money* [1936]) was a Marxist influenced by Thorstein Veblen and a disillusioned Whitmanite, a patriot-critic putting American artists and intellectuals in closer touch with the people. *Manhattan Transfer,* denounced as "an explosion in a cesspool" by Paul Elmer More, a leader of the older generation, was for F. Scott Fitzgerald and Sinclair Lewis a memorable event in American fiction. Expanding his focus in the trilogy that became *U.S.A.*, Dos portrays the fabric of a society in which many are corrupt or victimized. Praised by Sartre in 1937 as technically "the greatest writer of our time," his place beside Hemingway, Fitzgerald, and Faulkner was solidified by this volume classed with the great European novels for readers in 1930s. Its collectivist style influenced Mailer, Capote, and other novelists, and their imitators in documentary journalism, including George Packer's brilliant *The Unwinding*—in this anthology Packer calls "the great *U.S.A.* trilogy long overdue for a revival."

Dos Passos—who made the cover of *Time* when *The Big Money* appeared—was implausibly cast by the Communists as a hero of proletarian literature in the early thirties, then succeeded by John Steinbeck during the Popular Front. In the Spanish Civil War, between these dates, his ideology was abruptly changed by the fate of his friend and translator Jose Robles, a professor of Spanish at Johns Hopkins who also spoke Russian and became chief aide to Russian General Vladimir Gorev, head of Soviet military police in Spain. Robles was kidnapped and murdered, in secret, by the Russians or their allies. Long haunted by Robles's demise, Dos Passos would attack the New Deal tradition as an anti-Communist allied with Barry Goldwater and William F. Buckley. I asked my mother about his shifting politics and the bitter aspect of his chronicles after the forties. "He was never bitter when I knew him," she said, and although sometimes rueful, his letters and notes to her, like his later fiction, are heartfelt.

When Mother died in 1995, I read through their correspondence from 1922 through 1929, including her letters after returning to Texas from Strasbourg, which she'd had him send back. The pair spent only scattered hours together after four to five weeks in the summer and fall of 1924, and letters tell their story better than could our technology of cell phones and instant messaging. They round out a tale of young love frustrated by inexperience, by circumstance and timing. The story complements Crystal's accounts of her first exhilarating weeks in Paris and Strasbourg, and Dos's unpublished narrative of his thirteen-day hike through the Pyrenees into France. As an editor, I have made cuts in Mother's long letters and sometimes reordered Dos Passos's shorter ones for clarity and momentum. Though their letters are seldom dated and dates on the envelopes sometimes blurred, the situation is plain to see. Dos learned his trade, working out his identity as he captured life on the page, while Crys (his name for her) pursued the Ph.D. she hoped would help her teach in a university in future. A duty to herself became identified with that to the doting, oppressive father who paid the bills. Dos had no money, living off advances and

Preface

xv

loans from editors, with handouts from his mother's sister, the Aunt-Protectoress Auntie Mame (Mrs. James Riely Gordon).

His and Crystal's exchanges when she returned to Texas have an operatic sweep, with ascending climaxes until my mother's engagement to Lewis Dabney in 1926 and their marriage the following year. Crys and Dos maintained their affection, loyalty, and mutual respect through her marriage and his two, to women about whom he wrote to her. That the friendship survived into old age speaks well for all involved. As I absorbed a correspondence that was seventy years old when it came to me, the greater discovery for a son who knew his mother wrote good letters was her review of *The Sun Also Rises* followed by the second volume of Hemingway's stories in the *Dallas Morning News* in 1927. Neither is listed in Hanneman's *Comprehensive Bibliography of Hemingway*. Edmund Wilson hadn't known there was any good criticism when he was writing about early Hemingway, as he told me when I edited his journals during the 1960s. Neither Hemingway nor Dos Passos knew of Crystal's pieces when they appeared.

Although my mother learned a refined French at the University of Strasbourg, she was educated by American writers in Paris. Hemingway took her to tea with Gertrude Stein, on the walk there praising Stein's brains in the same term she used in a 1924 letter to Wilson. He introduced her to Ezra Pound in a café. Briefly back from Italy, the poet mentioned a second great piece by Eliot but said nothing of having remade *The Waste Land,* as the world learned when the typescript turned up in John Quinn's papers at the New York Public Library. She and Dos spent an evening with his close companion E. E. Cummings in New York. The Fitzgeralds visited Paris during her seventeen days there in May 1925. She was with Hadley and Zelda while the men brought back the topless convertible from Lyon, and she heard Hemingway report in person on this escapade, not quite the same version offered in *A Moveable Feast.*

My mother eventually outlined her and Dos Passos's story for his biographers. Townsend Ludington saw the correspondence at Virginia, knew a lot of the early life and work wasn't in the record as he planned *John Dos Passos: A Twentieth-Century Odyssey* (1980). A chance conversation of one of his graduate students at the University of North Carolina at Chapel Hill with my cousin Lucy Ross put Ludington on Mother's track. She returned to their story in a telephone interview with Virginia Spencer Carr for *Dos Passos: A Life* (1984). ("We were sweethearts," she explained, using the homely phrase.) Crystal barely registers as Dos's "girlfriend" in Michael Reynolds's volume on Hemingway in Paris (1989), but Hadley had loved the younger woman and taken her under her wing. Crystal made her contribution to the record as a vital source for Gioia Diliberto's *Hadley* (1992).

In offering my account of this story, I have the benefit of Ludington's detailed biography, which sketches their relationship as Mother described it at seventy-six, six years after Dos's death. There are carbons of Crystal's early letters to her family, and after Hemingway's death in 1962 she made notes for me ("for Lewis"), extending memories of Paris, Pamplona, and Strasbourg. The appendices in this volume contain Crystal's Hemingway pieces in the *Dallas News*. Included there too are Dos Passos's 1939 letter to the *New Republic* about Robles and the Spanish Civil War; and a letter from Crystal to Dos in their later years.

The selves the young man and woman present in their letters and early writing reflect the energy and independence associated with expatriates of the twenties. "When one marries one can no longer utterly be free," Crystal high-mindedly told herself after meeting the second man in her life to whom she could imagine being married. Identifying freedom with Dos Passos, in my father she chose someone who preferred the word "unhampered" in a letter that, cited in the appendices, shows his perceptiveness and common sense. He too was an intellectual, a great reader, and they were witty and charming together. Each drank too much, like others of their time and place. Both their sons became English professors, and a lingering rivalry between us distressed our parents, as we matched our heritage to different temperaments and abilities. Father was a classic type out of the old republic, Mother an original, a child from the American West and Europe, as these met in the modernism of her youth. I cannot be neutral about how John Dos Passos's engagement to her turned out, for if their profound compatibility had carried the day, these letters would be less moving, and I would not be here to introduce them.

PART I

Dos and Crys

ON AN EARLY SPRING day in 1923, Crystal Ross, herself almost twenty-three, sat in a Ford cabriolet before an overflowing creek in Caldwell County, Texas, typing a letter on the portable machine in her lap. Setting the scene, she described herself "reined in before a rushing stream of maple syrup waiting for it to dwindle and let us by. The roads are slick and puddly from melting snow and last night's rain. Left Lockhart about noon. We're only nine miles out of Austin now." The car and typewriter were gifts of her father, as was the pearl-handled pistol beside her, which she used when threatened by a rattler. She had graduated summa cum laude from the University of Texas in 1921, taken a master's at Columbia with a thesis on Machiavellian men in Elizabethan drama, and returned to Texas as a teaching assistant. Her apprenticeship in the great world of art and thought was beginning.

She relished the thirty-mile drive between Lockhart and Austin, her two major milieus. "Leaving the family group in assorted attitudes about the garage is a queer pang even in repetition," she typed, "but dragging across the tracks and thru Negro town and out to the hills is the transition":

As we swing along Clorinda [Crystal named her cars] hums and I
sing and we pour private thoughts inside ourselves, and half-marvel

Crystal Ross, circa early 1920s. (By permission of the estate of Lewis M. Dabney III)

that here we are real, grown, in a long skirt with a right jaunty cape, taking the long brown road wherever we choose [she has been reading *Leaves of Grass*]. We get all mellow with cheap philosophy and there is Austin. For a few miles we have a kind of homing lilt. Then as we narrow and dribble thru traffic we remember that we do not choose, and we become a commonplace, snub-nosed coupe and a commonplace young woman—lonely and idiotic.

She was writing to John Dos Passos, whom she had met six months before at the funeral of his Harvard classmate Wright McCormick, who had become her friend when teaching at the University of Texas. Wright "tumbled off a mountain down in Mexico," Dos recalled in dedicating to "Mickey" the early prose and verse published in *Rosinante to the Road Again*. He was now struggling with his second novel, *Streets of Night*, begun in college. Crystal told him, "I love, just love to ride this Middle Buster with Clorinda," seeing her life as a bucking bronco she could manage. The man who in *U.S.A.* would find the nation in "the speech of the people" replied, "Onion Creek and the Middle Buster are fine mouth-filling names. I envy you them."

From childhood Crystal had been a reader, often knowing what words meant before she heard them used. She had thought that "idiot"—as in "a commonplace young woman, lonely and idiotic"—was pronounced "idoit." "Something you read about," begins a notebook entry on Conrad's "Youth," written as though in Marlow's voice. "Here I am in a moment of exultation," she exclaims. "It is my first voyage as second-mate and I am only 20. O youth the strength, the faith of it, the imagination of it!" Her love of life impressed Burton Braley, a ballad collector who met her in New York and visited Lockhart. "To youth, joy, and Crystal—may they continue synonymous," Braley wrote inscribing a book to her. Her comment on Conrad invokes "endeavor, the test, the trial of life—looking anxiously for something out of life—that while expected is gone—unseen, in a sigh, in a flash—the youth, the strength, the romance of illusions." Crystal's romanticism, too had a dark side.

Her life was shaped by her father, a country doctor and a product of the frontier, severe and resolute. A. A. (Alonzo Alverley) Ross's people had come from Scotland to Missouri and then Texas after Bonnie Prince Charlie's failure at Culloden. Born in 1868 (he died in 1957), at thirteen he had been the breadwinner among orphaned children raised by their eldest sister, Crystal's formidable Aunt Stella. In that year his eyes were operated on without anesthetic, unsuccessfully. Two years later he went through the procedure again; this time the operation was pain-free (cocaine had come in as a topical anesthesia) and successful. He took a medical degree at Tulane, then for three years left his wife and two small children to study medicine in Vienna, never doubting he'd return to Texas. A healer whose religion was Freemasonry, when established in Lockhart (population 3,731 in 1920) Doctor Ross thought it appropriate to attend the various churches in rotation, catching up on his sleep in a back pew. With his friends the Jewish merchant and Lockhart's Catholic priest he reviewed an anti-Catholic march of the Ku Klux Klan, in his rough voice pointing out the marchers' identities beneath their sheets. "Doctor," his name in the family, was a Democrat and an early backer of young Lyndon Johnson, who wrote him a birthday letter every year. He hovered over the four children who came in pairs, Abner Jr. ("Bubba" or "Brudge") and Crystal Ray, Zerilda and Raleigh—hard on his sons, ostensibly indulgent of his daughters. The sons, who revered him, became doctors and in 1952 prevailed on him to join them in voting for Eisenhower, who campaigned against "socialized medicine." Yet in that same year Doctor confided to a grandson that Stevenson was "the biggest man in America." Crystal he called "the smartest girl who has ever been raised in this county and the best educated." Never close to her mother, she recalled playing in the garden as a girl while Mimma, who was overweight and had a bad heart, peered down through the curtains. She would eventually claim her father's place at the center of the family correspondence.

Dos Passos, growing up in a marginal position within his mother's extended family, was shy and socially ill at ease, yet congenial with other loners. Cummings thought him sexually repressed and a puritan. After their hike through the Pyrenees in 1919 the poet reported to Wilson—whom he also deemed repressed—that Dos thrashed and groaned in his sleep, sometimes waking him. When Estlin asked if he'd been dreaming about sex, he answered it was of wild swans flying overhead. When asked again about his dreams, Dos replied (Cummings exaggerating his slight lisp), "why I dweamed I had a bunch of aspawagus and was trying to give it to you." The comically homoerotic image—all three men had read Freud—silenced the poet, Wilson notes when setting this down in *The Twenties*. Hugo Bamman, drawn from Dos Passos, is uncomfortable at the fashionably bohemian Greenwich Village parties sketched in *I Thought of Daisy* (1929). He finds a place for his hat near the door to ease his departure whether to a rented room or to the docks, taking ship for Paris or the Middle East with all he needs in a musette bag. Although aggressively leftist, Hugo recoils from the New Women whose unconventionality he professes to admire but whom he cannot consider ladies.

Crystal's intensity, vivacity, honesty, her gutsiness on the page and in person appealed to Dos Passos. A flapper and something of a daredevil, in a fashionable photograph of 1925 she comes through as direct and earnest. A strong swimmer—she swam the Mississippi in her teens and the Hudson when at Columbia in 1921–22—she was given to diving into the unknown, and the Christmas after they met at McCormick's funeral sent Dos a card and a volume of cowboy poetry. Thanking her, he predicts that "the good ones like Frankie and Johnnie" will have been censored to meet the taste "of Mr. Sumner" [the head of the Anti-Vice Society]. He wonders what to do with Wright's papers. There is a novel that seems "too much in the embryo to do anything with" and some verse "that I think would be worth preserving. Though god knows it's little enough preservation to be flung into the dead festered ocean of the printed page. Isn't it madness this desire to preserve, preserve, mummify, embalm, can oneself one's friends one's loves and hates? Preserve for what?"

Resenting though he did having to "can" experience, Dos couldn't help but make the literary life attractive: "New York's snapping cold, and varnished and shiny and at sunset it's just grand. Have you read Eliot's 'Waste Land' in the last *Dial* [November 1922]? I like London Bridge is falling down falling down falling down and Phlebas the Phoenician." He wrote again after distressing news from her:

Isn't Dengue fever hideously painful? I've heard that it is—tough luck. I'd expected you'd be convalescing at the Lafayette. Honestly it hasn't been the same since you left it.

The first of the year was a most marvelous crystal day. Sky ice green with mare's tails and occasional blotting gray sleet-storm blindness, across the bright zero sunlight. Page the omen [this would be one of Crystal's pet phrases]. Here's luck to you.

A postscript addresses her interest in studying abroad: "If the foreign university were an excuse it would be fine—the Sorbonne (alias Paris) or Grenoble (Savoy mountains) or Cambridge (London fog)—but haven't you been rather a lot in universities Crys? Why not a grand tour? But you seem to be fairly busy gulping impressions where you are." Phi Beta Kappa at Texas and Columbia, the young woman replied, "You're right I've been a lot in universities":

Teaching's my trade—a funny trade it is, too, guaranteeing youth to the old and age to the young ones. I'm three-hundred-and-eighty-two and a fraction myself. I writhe and am careful to be a good teacher. The students who "get me" are lucky. It isn't so mutual. Death!—the papers I have graded with sympathy! Yet the students are *alive*. I have a notion that "education" could be something broader and more liberal than a senseless scramble for grades and units.

In March Dos wrote as if to demonstrate the self-sufficiency for which she yearned:

I'm on the *SS ROUSSILLON* ex of the German China service and we are bowling along splendidly with the devil's own wind out of the southwest in our tail. Great combers pursue and foam along the stern and send long spiteful tongues along the decks and the boat groans and staggers and wallows on eastward.

Imagine Spring. I was so afraid it would come before I'd extricated myself from New York. The "Runnin' Wild Blues" were not what I wanted at that moment. I don't know why I'm going toward France rather than toward New Orleans, but it's probably that prices being equal I decided I'd have one fling in Europe before my money gave out (not forgetting the blessed exchange). From then on I shall pass it up for good and cultivate only the dark continents–America, Africa, Asia—and after all I think that darkness is more satisfying than a succession of light candle-power standardized bulbs.

Sometime in the summer I'm coming back to roam about the U.S. somehow—then I want to go to Mexico. I'm not going to live in New York again until I have a gray beard that reaches to my knees. It's a damn squirrel cage and I don't like the other squirrels. But boats are not made for thinking, they are made for forgetting.

He shares his literary enthusiasms, as Dos liked to in correspondence: "Have you read *Moll Flanders* & *The Fair Roxana?* I think Defoe's a whiz. Take care of yourself and your totem pole [the Middle Buster] and write me now and then—wow we took a roll there—care *Norton Harjes et Cie, 14 Place Vendôme Paris France.*" Here was a magnet and model for a precocious young woman needing a break from home.

A Texas Expatriate

IN HER NEXT LETTER Crystal has made her move:

Noon. Dos you Buggah! By the seven mad gods of the sea, I have just
received and accepted—by wire—a scholarship in the University
of Strasbourg for '23–'24—a shock—a compromise—but being
disinherited and disillusioned, I am not proud. I started to apply
for it, filled in blanks *de* birth and education, but when I found the
requests for recommendations, I balked. Hence, surprise, it's in
Comparative Lit. Pays tuition, lodging, a rebate of 3070 on passage
over and return plus 2,000 francs! Just—but in my present state,
it's a channel of blessing. I am dumb in French, ignorant of
German, and about medium minded I guess. I foresee weak-kneed
innuendoes and deeply hurt family protest, but I'm going to try
the surf.

Where in geography are you? Don't you want to be a link? Go
to Strasbourg and wait for me. September. Or be sure to arrive in
New York before I leave. In the name of those seven mad gods,
be a comfort to me. I'm scared. Shall I take the totem pole? Poor
Clorinda—and Dad just arranged so that I can't sell her!

She closes as they often would, "Be nice to yourself." Confronting her father's opposition—though he hadn't seriously threatened to disinherit her—she tells Dos, "You *are* a comfort to me, just being you. Crystal."

From Paris Dos momentarily doubts her choice of location:

> To think of you in Strasbourg—to think of an extraordinarily explosive creature like you in that funny musical comedy town, a French town pretending to be German, a German pretending to be French, with its limping cathedral and its vaudeville clock and its *pâté de fois gras* and its last surviving stork's nest—it's wonderful to conceive. I just can't picture it—and honestly it's a very pleasant place—I was stationed near there in the ambulance service for a while. However as Strasbourg will probably be a mere hub for your European wheel, I say go to it. I think it's fine. As a point, a fulcrum for that famous lever, or as a watch tower from which it's possible to survey the decay of civilizations and the course of empire, etc., the taller tower of the Strasbourg cathedrals is a damn fine place.

He takes note of a misadventure when diving into a Texas quarry, for which she had been hospitalized: "For god's sake Crys—even for the sake of having psychic experiences don't go knocking any more chunks out of that very well shaped anatomy of yours. I suppose our bodies are the graveyards of dead people we have loved. Knock a chunk out and you get a temporary resurrection." She expands on her plight, one that would require a second operation three years later: "Beg to report that wound quiescent, packed with a very smelly press. I prithee God, do not let me giggle—nor the wind to blow." He is ready to pursue her:

> Lawse I wish I could connect with you somewhere. That time in New York I was not compos at all. I was in the middle of a rather futile cyclone which has since, thanks to travel exercise white wine of Frascati and the contemplation of the mighty dead dispersed,

Noon — Dos, you Buggah! By the seven
mad gods of the sea — I have just received
and accepted - by wire - a scholarship in the University
of Strasbourg for '23-'24.   A check — but
a compromise — but being diminished and
disillusioned, I am not proud
to apply for it, filled in blanks of birth and
education. but when I found the requests for
recommendations, I balked.   Hence, surprise —
Its in comparative Lit —   not   paying tuition,
lodging, a rebate of 30% on passage — over, and return
and 2000 francs !   Just — but in my present
state, it's a channel of blessing.   I am
dumb in French, ignorant of German, and
about medium minded I guess. — I foresee
week-kneed in misdeeds! — deeply hurt family
protest, — but I am going to try the
curs.   Where in geography are
you ?   Don't you want to be a link?
Go to Strasbourg and wait for me. September —
In the name of those seven mad

Letter from Crystal Ross to John Dos Passos informing him of her acceptance into the doctoral program at the University of Strasbourg. (Albert and Shirley Small Special Collections Library, University of Virginia; by permission of the estate of John Dos Passos) leaving me in an oyster-like calm. I don't know where I'll be in September—probably in New York to speed the parting Strasbourger.

I'm in Paris, desperately trying to polish up a novel—Christ it's dull—that's coming out in August. Going to the Bay of Biscay to sun myself and swim. Write Norton Harjes, 14 *Place Vendôme* Paris.

She replies:

I think of you at the Bay of Biscay. And desperately polishing a novel whose theme and whose subject I know not.

You're a whiz and a whooping comfort and you too think the Strasbourg idea is funny. Academic congratulations have about strangled me. And I have to reciprocate—over the novel or the Bay of Biscay—but I'm bloomin' ignorant of you. So having nothing intelligent to contribute I prattle of myself, a subject to be avoided. I almost pop with the things I can't share here.

That bleeding side was a lingering interest. Incisions and stitches and a month of congealed motions. I limp now when I can remember to, but my self-respect was restored by the discovery of a rusty plowshare on the bottom of that pool. It is better to wreck a corkscrew dive on an accidental plowshare than agin a permanent rock.

After correcting the proofs of *Streets of Night* Dos Passos returned to New York and saw her off for France. Letters to him dramatize the new life. One is from the *Rochambeau,* a ship known to nearly every young expat of these years, whence Dos had written to her a few weeks before. Dating her letter September 21, 1923, she is *"sur le pont, mer houleuse"* (on the bridge, with a troubled sea). "A line a swell—Dos you came true beautifully, if briefly," she writes, adding: "They lived happily but not forever. Being but people. And the radiogram was a delicious angle in the contour of my departure on this my maiden voyage! Here begins the sea that ends not till the world's end." Sensible beyond her years, the country girl knows that what may be love is impermanent, and brings to her first encounter with the ocean a sense of mortality from her reading:

> I am glad I'd had some recent tucks taken in my soul else it would have burst with this exhilaration of personal emancipation and mystic vibration with the sea. The split soul. Tra la. Remember the peculiar snow-white forehead of Moby Dick? I saw him—just then.
>
> I like the passengers—queer postures they are: French families, a Lithuanian, Russian writer of memoirs, Italian designer, Indian convalescent (looks like Jesus), handsome Argentine agriculturalist (?), American artist of California landscape (we are passing the OLYMPIA), student musicians—other students of various dimensions and degrees of mental and Baedeker preparedness (ahem), Parisian lawyer, male Spanish dancer, and lots of children, one adorable little brown-eyed girl who has made all the week sweeter. I like the passengers, I listen in on all occasions and curse the American monogloty (*permettez*), but I prefer the crew—mysterious children of the everlasting sea, everlasting children of the mysterious sea—I love it. Funny limitless limited world. Steady old silhouette, the *ROCHAMBEAU*—wood and steel and junk welded into grace and stability. Funny how she never stops for breath—never *gathers* energy but just oozes along making a life as she goes—creating, discarding—going somewhere but not protesting arrival.

From this female image of life, she turns to Dos Passos and his plans:

> And you are going to revolutionize your way of living—of being daily that is? After Rockaway a little, a very little colony in the country, fresh eggs and worn furniture—a veranda and a vegetable garden. Too haphazard to be facetious? Save me a place as housekeeper. I've always wanted to keep house for a colony—on the side—in just

the adequate selfless way. Wow, what a roll [see "wow we took a roll there" in Dos's March letter, p. 9]. I've been *un peu malade* on the sly, and I'll always be a better girl for it. This grand old cradle has patched my threadbare sleep with a magic blue fabric flecked with silver, and the salt air has healed *ma figure* [face] *abusée, confuse*. I was so glad to get away from New York and Austin, even Lockhart. I was tired and hobbled and microscopic. You could see that. The domestic wrench had left me physically numb and mentally maudlin.

"I think that my program is selfish—and cruel in parental perspective," she proclaims in a voice like Stephen Daedalus in Joyce's *Portrait of the Artist*:

> The only conceivable purpose of existence demands that every unit shall come to its fullest self-realization and the way to this selfhood is across the chasms of tradition and convention—by day, like the pathway of unbearable orange radiance across the sea to the sun—by night the phantom white moon fire on the same sea. A day at a time and illusion thru disillusion. That's the pattern. Probably all rot but I've got a sort of concept sketching and I can remember Dad and yet contemplate Strasbourg, the cream of the compromise. To the new life! Tell me how yours goes.
>
> Be nice to yourself. You forgot to tell me some edges about Paris, but I'll be pretty busy with the middles I guess. Oh come on to Germany in the Spring. Let's go to Norway. The dark continents will persist. That Atlas is a joy—I've traced a route whereby I can progress home in stages across the Pacific, in a future haze. Had more fun crossing the Red Sea.
>
> In Paris I'll live at 4 *Rue de Chevreuse*—or *Chartreuse*—I'm cheerfully at sea but I favor the former. In Strasbourg I have faith that the university will take care of me. Won't you send me a proof of the book? It's nice to have you materialize. I liked the lunch.
> Crys

Last Day Out. England looming. A maiden voyage is a wonderful thing. I never really breathed before. I want to be a seagull and sleep on a cresting wave. I am a seagull, but I'm not sleepy yet.

Three months later, in a Christmas letter to Dos from Strasbourg, Crystal recalls the Paris weeks that were her first taste of Europe. Echoing Twain's *Innocents Abroad,* she anticipates Gershwin's version of their generation's affair with the City of Light:

The month in Paris was glorious and awful—the richest and the loneliest in my life. Every morning I was born a different person, amplified and frightened by the day before. I was glad I was still young enough to be suffocated with internal enthusiasm. In Strasbourg one dares to express it, but there my experience was purely objective. Things flowed over me thru and by me in a great golden sweep. On the five and six days of every glorious week of sunshine and chrysanthemums I was glad to be an atom, a molecule, a drop in the golden rush. And now I possess Paris—in perfect alliteration. Bought a compass to find my way about and hiked all over the place—crisscross, around and straight thru, miles a day and gallons of beer and coffee on the side walk (I hate beer—except Strasbourg dunkel). My stockings came down and I didn't even try to pull 'em surreptitiously. I left the loveliest things in the windows without an impulse toward possession, and walked thru the Tuileries at dusk bare headed and forgot I was being followed by a delightful little man, shriveled and dapper. I went in to every Cathedral to pray and discovered after three weeks of such worship that I was crossing myself backwards. Then I tried a confessional to regret the holy water I had wasted, but I hadn't the courage to go through with it even in an unknown tongue. I did the suburbs and chateaux on sunny days, the flower market every day and the bird market on Sunday and the museums when I had the courage and could escape without the logical accompaniment of my spinster

friends. O yes I lived in the Latin quarter round the corner from The
Dome and the Rotonde in an old, old house [the University Women's
Club, 4 *rue de Chevreuse*] with a court and a garden, a sort of tall gray
silk hat street.

Leaving Paris was a desolation. I was scared to death and had
larned no French in spite of the theatre. But it was comparatively
easy technically. I did sit with perfect poise for half an hour on the
wrong train, only to be removed with baggage by a middle-aged
porter who suspected me of a destination—the coach wasn't going
nowhere that day. But at last there was Reims where I had intended
to stay a few hours and stayed several days instead, having picked
up a perfectly nice—love the phrase, don't you?—American man of
Annapolis background and watch fob. There was lots of champagne
and I got away with the rather cheap adventure without the aroma of
being my father's daughter—tho I can't forget how I loathed myself
in the hang-over, and probably won't risk it again. The outlying
Frenchmen rather wither one's girlish illusions. O Dos it was awful.
I hit the bottom so flat, and depths I hadn't dreamed of. It was after
Metz and Verdun, and still with the hangover. For a long time in
Paris I hadn't slept, [and] on that cold dark train too drunk to sit
up but sober enough to think, the only joy I could generate was
the wrong side of the fun I had just had: my certainty that I'll live
but once.

From the security of a new home in Strasbourg she adds, "If I get much
colder I won't live that long," Sitting by her brown porcelain stove, she
wonders if he has a fireplace in New York. "Dos dear one, the boy I left
behind me, Douglas, dear Douglas, sweet William and so forth," she
asks. "What are you doing or are you thinking?" She entertains as an
American innocent:

I live at one *quai* Dietrich, in the foyer *universitaire* (no one knows
what a foyer is). Men and women and married couples live here in

rubber pigeonholes bulging back and forth into each other. We are all cheerfully mixed as to gender, and drifting the corridors in negligee is always a hazard. And all my money has been stolen in three lots; so that now I see some justification for the kilograms of keys I carry about with me, this for the iron gate, this for the corridor and this for the lift, if it works. The head porter was arrested for stealing last week and is back again today. But he is my best friend. The night I came in from the station with two trunks and three-to-ten hand packages and was emptied out of the taxi provided by the police department for my distress, when we, the Lockhart embassy, were all spilled out there in the court, the porter came to see what the splatter was about. I tried intelligently enough to tell him my name. Ross in his dialect signifies horse, so he thought I wanted a horse. My entire beautiful name I translate in Alsatian as Miss Cutglass, Skate-Fish, Horse: there, that is your Christmas present.

Strasbourg—I love it, shivers and midnight sun and all. I shall have been here two months Christmas if it rains every day this week and gets colder. It is the most absurd little town in the world, isn't it? and the loveliest. How did it ever happen to these absurd Alsatians? And how did they happen? I shall stay here forever I think and follow the funny little streets, and tell over the things in the windows, sausages and cheeses and chocolate Santa Clauses and carrots made of almond paste, and little naked candy pigs for good luck and seventeen-hundred varieties of corsets displayed in pink, yellow, lavender, even black and gold, but never worn. One of my favorite games—and I could write an anthology on *solitaires*—is trying restaurants and taverns and brasseries after this fashion. Having taken stock of the menu and the atmosphere, mostly I say gentle foreign little regrets and exit in all leisure. It's fun to try shops the same way, and find that you have lost or left your purse, or promise to search out a friend who speaks the language and return—the future tense just stumps me tho—and I have caught myself at this game to the extent of an amazing array of queer vegetables and toys and little buckets and even raw sausages. I bought a trick monkey for you at the trick toy store, where I and all the little gamins of Strasbourg go every evening to see them light up the awful eyes of their prize tiger and set his tail on its electrical wagging. But I like the monkey so well and know so little about you that I am keeping it for a household god. It is named Oscar–after you—and expands with temperature. So would I, if there were any.

Strasbourg—comic opera is right. You tried to tell me, but I couldn't conceive of it. A contrast to take your breath on every corner, until you get used to being breathless and work out your catalogues of things French, things German, and things hybrid. The university is idiotic utterly—they sent some good professors here to get it started and then took them away—but the student body is cosmopolitan on a private scale, and as such absorbing. I have the distinction of being the premiere danseuse among the coed-*demoiselles,* having won a prize in a *concours* of two weeks worth of evenings and accompanying foot aches, my partner, cavalier, a Beethoven-headed communist, a veritable Alsatian and adorable. But, being the *première danseuse,* I am swamped with offers of linguistical instruction and theatre tickets and soirees and other local exercises. It was the tango that decided the jury and the student rooting section, and I am still wondering what the tango is all about. It is for this that we have scholarships to France.

But the municipal baths, it is there I really have my being. I perched here until I got unbearably dirty and then essayed the *Grands Établissements de Bains de la Ville de Strasbourg*—and remained to pray! German-built they are and the most admirable institution in all of Europe I know. There are baths medicinal and hydro-electric and Turkish and ordinaire, and there is a wonderful white-tiled and ample swimming pool, deep enough too, and spring-boarded with showers in booths along the wall. I bought a season ticket immediately, and since the day I dived into the pool from the first-class balcony, a thing expressly forbidden in two languages, I

have been Queen of the Municipal Baths. It gives me something to
live for, and that I need. Outside my mind, which is muddy.

Anyway life is to spend, to keep moving with, it is all a process anyway,
that's what I have learned from this novelty and isolation and a little
edge of experience [in] *la belle* France: buying carrots in the morning
perhaps, and reaching after material you simply do not grasp and
eating with strangers who shout with laughter because you put salt
on an apple and freezing at night, and having above the substratum
of health and well-being, vague Lydia L. Pinkham symptoms, and
meeting every French emergency with one of three expressions. That
is living one's own life and I find it damn good, and ride the world
from this angle. I think I shall be even with the universe after a little
concentration, and ready to look at things straight—clear-visioned if
it breaks me. O it is fun to find that one has the fiber—and if the piper
comes and demands his pay I shall just follow him on to Hamlin.

Slapstick again softens her dark realism:

Merry Christmas, if you like. I am broke myself, destitute and almost
barefoot, having put my shoes in the oven to dry and burned 'em to
cracklings. Have just returned from the opera—*Tristan and Isolde,*
where the communist conveyed me to a box and I wore hockey shoes
and simulated a sore foot. The theatre here is fun. Their comedies
break the speed limit as burlesques and the municipal music is
distinctly good. But the Alsatian fetes are nicest. I have a costume
and take part in all the street dances. They let the Germans come
back across the Rhine for Memorial Day services.

Business here is dying, the canals are filling up since the French
insist on buying German products only through the additional
expense of Swiss exchange. My friends tell me that the German
professors and their families are living on noodles, and the Youth
Movement frets and rebels and wear sandals to prove their point.
I'd like to visit their colony [at] Christmas, but am loathe to leave

Strasbourg, afraid it will float away while I am gone. For it does float, like Ivory soap, in any medium, in geography, politics, linguistics, culture, religion. It Floats.

She returns to her opening summons:

Dos, you must come over to Strasbourg, the town of the ways, do you hear, *la ville des rues*—you must come over. I promise not to be so voluble. *Il faut que vous*—o what a triumph—write me immediately, all your symptoms mental, physical and emotional. Won't you? I *am* lonely.
Crys

A Rover on the Road

RELISHING THIS LETTER AND its shipboard predecessor, Dos asks her to "send me more in spite of my shortcomings in the answer line." He sketches his life to the latest battle against near-sightedness:

> I've been having the ultimate Waterloo with my eyes. Extraordinary to relate, Napoleon instead of escaping in a *landau* is charging the British squares—aided by General Bates' new system of relaxation and comic exercises, the ranks of Myopia are giving ground. *Vive l'Empereur!* and so I'm able to write a little and to read and to occasionally make out a sign all without either glasses or headaches—and I hope at the end of 6 months of very tedious exercise to be able to see a friendly face across the street. This alibi is disgustingly genuine, so lets not talk about it.
>
> Hot rum toddy—known as an *Américaine*—is what you need to keep you warm young lady. A liberating application each night before going to bed will tickle the toes of a nostalgic Texan with drowsy heat.
>
> Strange about your money being stolen—all these symptoms of decay are depressing—but I can't imagine thievery—not that it is of

any importance in itself in such a tight little town as Strasbourg. A Ballade of the Lustige Widow ought—to be written about our young heroine—*La Reine des Bains Municipaux* [queen of the municipal baths]—in twenty tableaux & two acts.

As for symptoms, Crys—I'm living at 213 (address 214 Riverside for letters) in a small narrow vomit green bedroom ($5 week and 75 cents extra for a small gas asphixiator) and trying to work and to cure my eyes. I sit there most of the day and try to make novelistic fragments join into a whole. Two evenings a week I paint colored ladies of enchanting and glossy bulginess [sketch on margin]. Other times I mope about my last novel and my next but one and wonder about the strange antics of the implacable and, it is alleged, gilt-edged Aphrodite.

Leaving that subject to return in *Manhattan Transfer* and *U.S.A.*, he settles for the restless New Yorker's role:

Then I drink bad gin with friends and swallow tea from 5 to 12. And always I undergo the little nickel hysteria of New York—fire escape & steam ship whistles & ferryboats & Fourteenth Street & Second Avenue & Harlem. I've squabbled with all the literati and am going in a week or so—if I can sell a long account of desert travel—down to New Orleans for a month or two. In the summer I have a project of going to Moscow to work with the Kamerny Theater—if a certain combination produces the desired alloy ie mazuma chink, dough, iron men for transportation. And that's my symptoms. And I'm at sea and just turned 28—to the masthead Columbus—and there's no land ho and the crew is growing mutinous.

He is ready for action:

If I go to Russia where will you be, say in May, so that I can pay my respects (spot cash respects no checks or drafts accepted)?

A Rover on the Road

23

Berlin in May? Paris in May? Strasbourg in May? Once I had to
leave a dinner uneaten in a Strasbourg restaurant having only
money for the soup. Suppose we go and eat the rest of it. Gosh it
smelled good too. *Foie gras* in some *"imbilivible"* as Krazy [Kat—
a comic strip of the twenties] would say. Had a very pleasant dinner
with the Greeting [their friend Cabell Greet, who was writing his
Columbia dissertation and would teach medieval English literature
at Barnard]. I'm reading Freud—a great person. I like his picture and
anecdotes better than his theories. But *Interpretation of Dreams* is a
book that rings the bell.

Freud's vision of sexual horses at play in the psyche was becoming a
new organizing metaphor for American writers, Dos included. Looking
forward to hearing "more of Persephone's underground adventures,
O Helen of the *Bains Publiques*," he urges her to "Be good to Oscar my
monkey. I shall claim him some day."

Crystal would see their attraction as more intellectual than physi-
cal but was quite willing to play Persephone or Helen to such a man:
"Dos Darlink, Honey, if you only know all the dreams I've dreamed of
you Way Down upon the Swanee River far, far away / The Sun Shines
Bright on My Old Kentucky Home, T'is summer the darkies are gay /
O Susannah O Don't you cry for me, for I'm goin' to Louisiana wid
my banjo on my knee. Did you? I hope so. And the letter was Wealth!!
Thank you." It's spring, and she happily burns the candle:

This is the windy Sunday before Mardi Gras and nobody's
responsible! We danced all night at the *Bal des Artistes*—(masques
abandoned). O dear Pierrot, I did not know that dancing was so
sweet. Interesting psychology—losing identity. I'm trying to keep
awake for an *aperitif* rendezvous at the local *Café de la Paix* and
then Whoops! a hike into the villages to see the natives having
Carnival before *Carême* [Lent]. Meanwhile I'm installed amid an
array—*fantastique*—*tordante* [funny] *épouvantable* [terrible] of Sunday

gâteaux in rows and circles *chez* my favorite *patisserie* where you shall come for coffee in the month of May.

For heaven's sake, or the sake of the Black Forest or the eleven plaid gods of maidens who roam amid desolate mediocrity, make your combination come true. Make it. In May I will, can, could be most anywhere for 2–6 days but I should be in Strasbourg for the 7th day of most weeks! It might be lovely here then; perhaps loveliest. I plan to blossom like a prairie flower with returning sunshine. Every hour. O Dos, come thru, by, at, to but stay a month. You could live here cheaply, as cheaply, and work or play. Even clothing is beginning to easy up. And I've a friend who's just published his doctor's thesis, "The Stabilization of the Franc." Droll subject. I had 500 more stolen yesterday, but don't blame Strasbourg nor our nice though maddening Alsatians for my criminal carelessness. I'll find a place for you to live and I have a *merveilleuse* [marvelous] *spirituelle* but broad-bosomed *dame Française* to eat and sentimentalize with, an elegant *veuve* [widow] who lost her son in World War I.

I'm awfully glad over your eyes, and I know just the daily disgust of arriving toward slow startling peaks. So splice a few of the exercises with energy from me. Write me, quick, and come on over. If you can't make Strasbourg, tell me the nearest place, or the most interesting. I'm in a state—a shooting star state. Can't express to confide me [*sic*] autobiographical riots. Plan to be a meteor presently, cold in a field of celery roots—brownish black—but sulphury.

The meteor looks back to her seagull on mortality's cresting wave. As yet unfettered by a social role, Crystal's love of life is fed by everything around her:

Fun to be reading French—*épatante!* [marvelous]. You've forgotten how it is to come into a language and literature not English. It clears like water charged with chlorine and one looks through delicate crystal—there's the French of it—a fluid glass. O I've got so many gorgeous things to read. It's like bein' born agin! And just as raw.

O Dos we'll do a handstand in Place Kleber and *donnerons un coup de pied en arriére* [jump out of our shoes backward] at the Pasteur monument. Bring me three pairs of low-heeled shoes, a plain black wool bathin' suit size 18, a fur coat and some Woodbury soap! But your rhum remedy has saved Madame. I rest just a touch inebriated! But I got more than demi-soused (I'm grammatically feminine) at the *cuisiniers Grand Balle d'Alsace-Lorraine*. Hubsch the noble savage and I continue to collect tango prizes. He washes his hair in eau de cologne—*tellement* [rather] tricky that boy.

Hurry Dos: the fare from Paris to Leipsig is 1200 fr. and every fare goes up 40% the 15th. Hurry and get here so you can stay. I am having a *canard* [a shriek] for you this minute. Don't you let me do a poor Butterfly in Strasbourg.

As she'd tell her family, Dos would always be a rover—"he roves so simply and so well." She had moved too, a few hundred feet, was now boarding at 3 Quai St. Thomas, the home of the "elegant widow with a rose interior." Madame Eugenie Epp's character and household brought stability to the young American's life over the next sixteen months. In the case of relics in her front parlor, bridging the two cultures of Alsace-Lorraine, were the medal and military cap of one of Napoleon's marshals and Martin Luther's wedding ring, which Madame had loaned to friends needing respectability at the market when Strasbourg was German before World War I. She had been married at seventeen to a husband of thirty who died young. Her elder son, Alfred, a French officer out of St. Cyr, was killed at Chateau-Thierry, his body so mangled he was identified through what she called his "beautiful dentistry." Her younger son, Jean, who sometimes visited, was, Crystal wrote to Lockhart, "a charming boy about half as intelligent as she is, but the last word in Frenchiness and of the most perfect manners I have witnessed. He lifts the bread tray with the arm and quiet ease that a genius puts into a piano scale." There was also the maid Marie, whose struggles with romance, pregnancy, and a sometimes difficult mistress the American followed sympathetically.

Madame Epp had a French intellectual crispness. Of eighty-year-old Anatole France—whom she admired and who died that fall—she said, "*Il prit son temps pour mourir*" (he took his time dying). Yet she was a motherly soul, "a constant comfort" and anchor, useful in the chaperone's role. At college Crystal had had one or two crushes, alarming her father and older brother, and she could be burdened by the men she attracted—by Burton Braley the ballad collector and Hubsch, the Communist, pro-American like other radical students. A poet and the incarnation of romantic youth, Hubsch had a small landed inheritance but no money, and he sometimes fell into Werther's melancholy. "There was never on earth a nobler nature, nor a finer, a purer body," she reassured her family when Doctor Ross threatened to take ship to Le Havre and drag her home. Hessell, an Alsatian with a title, finished a scientific doctorate and passed the *soutenance* (defense of the dissertation) while pursuing what he called a study of the young lady. He was infatuated with her and would propose, he said, "after making my fortune in three years in America." When he finally got off to New York, determined also to get Crystal a job, Hessell presented her with a khaki shirt, leftover medicine and ink, shoes, the flowers and plants that filled his room, candy, fruit, and catsup.

In February '24 Dos Passos, who would be exposed to Madame Epp's household, wrote to her from bohemian New Orleans. He was escaping literary New York with an early version of *Manhattan Transfer* on his mind: "Whatho Crystabel? I'm at this moment chilly as a frozen clam, which made me think of you refrigerating in Strasbourg. I'm inhabiting a small raspberry and apricot-colored room with a cobalt blue bed in the dilapidated parts of New Orleans. It's splendid and [I'm] doing a lot of work and living like a hermit crab, but bum how chilly it is, as my room has no heat and costs $2.50 per week." His summers on Virginia's Northern Neck had made Dos, observer of American regional cultures, explorer of odd corners of the modern world, something of a southerner:

> Honestly I like your south. Things and people are wider and less perpendicular than in New York. I like the way the Mississippi flows above the town like a stream of molasses on a table. I like the preposterous boats that look like shoeboxes decorated with icing that navigate its turbid waters. I like the smell that comes off the sugar refineries in the evening. And now everything is heating up for Mardi Gras and everywhere is full of drinking and betting and crapshooting and horseracing and various pomps of Satan. I don't know anywhere one gets more genuinely the tang of our raw rattletrap continent than in Canal St.
>
> Look, do write me. I'm wondering what's become of you. You haven't dived into the Rhine and become a Lorelei have you? If all goes well, I'm booked for Russia in about May via Paris, Leipsig and whatever parts of the continent you will at that time be habiting. IF—but it's no use magnifying the iffiness of the proposition.
>
> By the way, I refuse not to be given a monkey, particularly an animated monkey. If that animated monkey is not come across with I shall consider myself grossly insulted. My landlady has a parrot named Murphy and the little puppy dog downstairs is called Romeo.
>
> Spring in the Vosges—drink a glass of *Liebfraumilch* for me & eat a wild strawberry or two.
>
> Yours Dos

A month later, the creator of Vag and other wanderers in *U.S.A.* tells of "walking down Florida, that Eden of real estate men and fake orange groves":

> Strangely enough I find pleasant backwoods roads, wild pigs splashing through swamp full of live oaks, mocking birds singing in every bough, a vast and beautiful beach where you never see a

human soul, only limousines and sedans, tightly closed, navigating the sands as if by their own volition. It's all like high life in the movies. It's the high point and ideal of our civilization, a snakeless Eden (mortgaged), with running water and concrete garage. Still the people you meet along the road have an almost idiot amiability that's most appealing and so many people offer you rides that walking is quite difficult.

Arriving "flat" and wiring for money that "has not forthcome," he haunts the telegraph office while his watch "is held in pawn for my hotel bill and my thoughts have been gloomy unmoneyed thoughts." He adds: "I've been stranded in many places, but never have I found it so uneasy and irksome as these last two days. It's as if red ants are crawling all over me and I can't keep away from the telegraph office. I'll go there now just on the chance":

Oh elegant just and mighty dollar. Oh hooray mazuma chink lettuce spinach spondulix! The tramp of the iron men is faintly audible over the telegraph wires; the day is saved—o cash where is thy victory? O small change where is thy stingalingaling?

Well finally my pockets comfortably stuffed with the blessed simoleons I left Daytona like a bat out of hell and continued for several splendid days till I finally boarded a freight in the town of Venice, Fla. and by devious routes arrived at West Palm Beach of Senatorial fame in a state of general collapse and acute sunburn, and there I am now lurking in a hotel waiting for a train to take me to Key West. I like the hilly western part of Florida with its lakes and its endless rows of strange trees. I couldn't seem to get into the Everglades as there isn't a road yet, the nearest I could get to them the mucky plains round Lake Okeechobee and a certain jumping-off place known as Moore Haven.

I still hope to be drifting through Strasbourg in about May—gosh that's next month, for this is the second of April. I'll probably find

some sort of definite news of the Russian expedition when I get to
Key West.
Take care of yourself, Dos
    My nose is like an overripe strawberry from the sun.

The insular independence of Key West, with its population of
English-speaking whites from the States and the Caribbean mixed
with Spanish and Cuban workers in the cigar factories, delighted him.
"The cigarrollers were interesting people to talk to, well informed and
also surprisingly well read," Dos reports. "They had a habit of hiring
someone to read to them at each long table while they worked—Socialist
newspapers, 19th century Spanish novels, translations of Dostoevski or
Tolstoi." This place that he relished also "suited Ernest to a T"—nobody
seemed to have heard of game laws or Prohibition—and to Hemingway
in Paris he called it "Provincetown but with no winters." A few years
later he would regularly visit the Hemingways there. Now he is intent
upon meeting up with the "nostalgic Texan":

Dear Crys,
I'm very anxious to undergo the extraordinary spectacle of CR
swimmer of the Hudson and Miss. Rivers, rider of the Middle Buster,
Sachemess of Alohaloha [her girlhood camp] etc. etc., in the grip of
the dilapidated but not quite dying continent of Europe. I suppose
that after laundering your spirits in the blued Mediterranean
you'll be back in Alsace to drink May wine and spring beer and to
shatter the already *fruhling* [Spring-broken] hearts of majors and
communists by the mellifluous dancing of the tango. I'm straining
at the bit. It's all a question of money as the man said who broke
the Bank at Monte Carlo. The Muscovite mirage has flickered out.
If I can collect a few pennies and allay certain debts I'll probably
sail early in June, but it's May 13th and everything is very vague.
However don't be surprised to see me turn up—after all one might
as well be dead broke in Europe as in New York. For Christ's sweet

sake don't disappear along with those two hundred a week the light-fingered Alsatians make off with.

I'm for a short time in my diggings of 3 Washington Square. It's pleasant to be in a big room where I can paint and not olive mantelpieces. It'll be nice to walk around in a Paris of which the grand panjandarum is no longer *Poincaré-la-Guerre*.

I feel like a keg of home brew that has been corked up too tight—Zowie. Take care of yourself and don't take any wooden nickels. Dos

My address will be 214 Riverside Drive [Aunt Mamie's address] and suddenly care Bankers Trust Company, *Place Vendôme Paris* (Please hold). But I'll write or wire any developments.

Paris and Pamplona in the Summer of 1924

BY JUNE HE IS in Paris:

Lookie Crys—would you like to come down here for a week? I could get you a room at 10–12 francs in this hotel that is very pleasant. I'd like to take you to Mr. Diageloff's [Diaghilev's] ballet [*Les noces*] and to Sceaux Robinson [an elegant railroad, redolent of the era of Proust, that in the twenties ran from the center of Paris to St. Germain, Neuilly, and other suburbs]. This is purely a selfish suggestion as I feel that a little of the air of the Middle Buster is needed to blow away the gray green silvery cobwebs. I'll return the visit to you in Strasbourg. If you don't feel like coming down, I'll come up and visit you in a couple of weeks. I want to see some people here and to see the Moscow man who is to appear *incessamente* as they say in the papers.

I want you to see *Noces,* so do try and find the idea of coming down pleasant. Wire me here, *Hotel du Pavillon, 6, rue de Verneuil* if and when. You ought to go to St. Germain too—and the *Foire* [Fair] *de Neuilly* is on. I bet you haven't been up the Eiffel Tower. I'm wiring too.

Dos

> I have a bathing suit & 2 cakes of Woodbury's soap. Would have
> bought shoes but did not know the size.

Three-plus months in Paris and Spain, followed by a week in Strasbourg and a weekend in London, were what these two would have of the Old World. The Texan who had hiked across the "golden rush" of Paris with a compass, reoccupied her room and bath at 4 rue de Chevreuse. It was a block from the crossing of the Boulevard Raspail and the Boulevard Montparnasse, and five minutes from the Hemingways' new flat over the sawmill on Notre Dame des Champs. She first met the couple on the terrace of the Closerie des Lilas, "where Jake Barnes drinks Pernod and describes its effects," she would write reviewing *The Sun Also Rises* in 1927. "Robust, hulking, handsome, vivid," "probably the slouchiest figure in *Montmartre*," Hemingway wore canvas shoes and a Basque beret summer and winter. "After an aperitif, we dined at La Vinge's and went to a wrestling match." Alongside the two novelists over the next eighteen months she saw firsthand the birth of American literary modernism and experienced some of its pangs. Without ever making this her subject, Crystal lets pieces drop, as when summing up her and Dos's story for Townsend Ludington and Virginia Carr or characterizing Hadley for Diliberto.

Her account of the Hemingways' household in Hadley's time matches others. They had a chemical toilet and no bathtub. They bathed in friends' apartments, using Crys's tub when she was in Paris. They were "absolutely committed to one another," she told Hadley's biographers. "I was quite startled [by their divorce] because I marveled at their cohesion." Dos's memoirs take the same view. Hadley was eight years older than her husband, a subject Crystal recalled the Hemingways discussing. "Someone of rare purity," she was "a totally natural person, clean, fresh, and straight," who "instinctively did the right thing." "How sweet she holds her baby—a stone-faced Madonna," the young Texan noted, offering a doctor's daughter's advice about

Letter from John Dos Passos to Crystal Ross inviting her to visit him in Paris. (Albert and Shirley Small Special Collections Library, University of Virginia; by permission of the estate of Lewis M. Dabney III)

Bumby. Diliberto cites Crystal's memory of how, after Hadley heated the water on the stove, the flowered wallpaper bulged from the steam when she poured the water into his little tub. Dos Passos recalls this scene in *The Best Times:* "We would stroll back through the five o'clock crowds to the sawmill, and help Hadley give Bumby his bath. Bumby was a large, healthy, sociable infant and enjoyed the whole business. He would be tucked in bed and, when a pleasant buxom French peasant woman who took care of him arrived, we would go out to dinner." Dos was soon to relish the domesticity of Gerald and Sara Murphy with their three little tow-headed children, two of whom wouldn't make it to adulthood: "I had never had a proper family life and was developing an unexpressed yearning for it."

The two novelists, who had met when tending "pulverized people," enjoyed a warm camaraderie. Crystal would look back at the pleasure they gave each other in these Paris days, long before the Spanish Civil War and the fallout over Robles's murder. They shared their struggles with prose at the Closerie des Lilas, drinking Pernod, she thought, though in Dos's memoirs it is "some such innocuous liquid as vermouth cassis." They read the Old Testament aloud, comparing favorite passages. For Dos, Hemingway fused the accent of the King James Bible with the terse language of cables in the interchapters of *in our time,* out that spring from Three Mountains Press. Dos predicted his friend would be the great American stylist, a thought that in *The Best Times* (1966) is attached to the expanded, capitalized *In Our Time* published in 1925 in New York.

Hemingway's breakthrough as a story writer in '24 was transforming for Americans in Paris. With a confidence-building ease he wrote eight of the best pieces in this collection and its successor, *Men without Women,* drawing them together through "Big Two-Hearted River" as Joyce had *Dubliners* through "The Dead." Crystal would recall the young American before popularity affected his mannerisms. He was "warm," with "happy, small, live eyes," and "modest." He "obviated [the] ego" apparent in his love of boxing—he was trying to teach Pound how to keep up his guard—"by *laughing* at himself." At moments Hem sounded like Donald Ogden Stewart or Robert Benchley. "My forte," she recalled—it seemed "odd"—was "to play lines and serve back." Her accounts of her first year in Europe show her well-suited to this. In a draft of *The Best Times* Dos Passos calls it "a period when life seemed comical to all of us," adding: "Nobody ever got so mad that some fresh crack didn't bring him around. We drank a great deal but only cheerfully. We carried things off with great fits of laughing."

For him as well, 1924 was a milestone. In the autobiographical fragment called "July" and published in the *Transatlantic Review* Jimmy Herf is an adolescent on a southern farm, among the same relatives to be caricatured in their lives on Riverside Drive in *Manhattan Transfer,* written through the winter and spring of '25. Ford had wanted something for his magazine, and when he sailed to New York to raise money for the *Review* asked Hemingway to edit the issue in which Dos Passos's piece appeared. "July" quite lacks the objectivity and reportorial clarity of *Manhattan Transfer,* the swirling structure of intertwined lives, the ear for how their generation spoke. Creating that style when engaged to Crystal, Dos owns it in the narrative portraits of *U.S.A.*

Before Paris these two had enjoyed each other's company for four or five hours over twenty months of letter writing. He said he was very fond of her, and she loved his lack of pretense, his fierce intelligence and sweetness. "At first I was not at all in love with him and said so," she ingenuously confided to her father, mother, and elder brother, called Bubba (and by her sometimes "Brudge"), when reporting from Strasbourg on their holiday. Yet this is a letter about a crush: "He is tall with beautiful brown eyes—without glasses now and, so near-sighted that you feel sorry for him. He is rather good-looking tho the trenches [where he worked in the Norton-Harjes Ambulance Service in World War I] did something funny to his hair and left him baldish—black hair." The rheumatic fever of Dos's childhood regularly recurred, yet he'd become a great walker, sometime mountain climber, and explorer of cultures: "He is very healthy—has an unfailing energy and appetite. Walks like a winged steamroller. Likes to swim but does not do

John Dos Passos in France, circa 1924. Photograph by Lucien Vogel. (Albert and Shirley Small Special Collections Library, University of Virginia; by permission of the estate of John Dos Passos)

it so well. Hops to music rather than dances but no one can deny the rhythm." He was "brilliant without an atom of pose" and called himself "a solitaire," a word Crystal now claimed for herself.

Guilelessly trusting her family, she told them Dos Passos seemed "absurdly my fate—the incarnation of all my old insistencies on a husband who would not husband one, a marriage that one could have and be without. Not a husband at all, but a sort of fellow explorer of the requisite sex." In this respect she was far ahead of her time. Sexually inexperienced, "when things began to happen and Paris was so crowded and cityish" she was "willing to follow the spark on the Spanish gleam." The couple left for the South of France and Pamplona, the Hemingways not far behind, having put the *Review* to bed. Dos Passos and Crys took a train via Nantes to Le Plessis to call on Germaine Lucas-Championniére, a writer about music and the stage, briefly a girlfriend, now a confidante. Crystal is one of four women in a faded photograph of a sack race, the novelist in a three-piece suit about to join them. Ludington's biography picks the couple up at St. Jean Pied de Port near the Spanish border. The next day they hiked through the pass at Roncesvalles, Crys struggling to keep up with the "winged steamroller." New shoes didn't help, and she was glad to complete the thirty miles to Burguete on a donkey. There the Hemingways found them, and the four went on to Pamplona, staying at the Hotel de la Perla, across the square from the Quintana, to be taken over by the *Sun Also Rises* crowd a year later. Hemingway had reserved a double room for Dos and Crys and was irritated when she demurred. They'd had separate rooms on the way down, and she took Donald Ogden Stewart's while Stewart moved in with Dos.

Hemingway, who had come upon the San Ferman fiesta in Pamplona in '23, was an aficionado when he set up the '24 expedition, to his mother calling it "a purely Spanish fiesta" with "practically no foreigners." That couldn't be said after Stewart and he risked their lives in the ring, wowing the crowd and making news in the American press. Stewart misunderstood the bullfighter's maneuver with his cape, called the veronica. He tried to move aside and was knocked down when the bull charged, tried again and had two ribs broken, was falsely reported to have been gored. In retrospect he thought himself cowardly rather than courageous, being full of wine and shamed into bravado by Hemingway, as well as, Stewart recalled, the presence of "the wives," Hadley and Sally Bird, who came with her husband, Bill, of Three Mountains Press. Stewart admired the way Dos, with no stake in his image as hunter or fisherman, shrugged off Hemingway's goading. Crys saw Hadley observe Hem's "brave absurdity" as, egging on the would-be bullfighters, he "stood up and demanded death for a *horse* [emphasis Crystal's]." The dark fate of horses, often gored when the picadors pricked the bulls with their lances, kept this Texan from enjoying the bullfight, despite its Spanish dignity.

Michael Reynolds's account of the arena in *Hemingway: The Paris Years* (1999) lacks Crystal's notes and minimizes the perspectives of Dos and Stewart. Dos grew impatient with the antics of friends whose free-flowing camaraderie he had enjoyed in Paris. Since Roncesvalles he had been praising the Spanish, and at Pamplona observed that they shared their wineskins in family groups, that the women didn't drink and dance in the streets like some of the American ones—he disapproved of Sally, recalled by Crystal as "a camp follower, a sweet actress." In *The Best Times* Dos says: "There were too many exhibitionistic personalities to suit me. The sight of a group of young men trying to prove how *hombre* they were got on my nerves." "The joke on me," this natural storyteller genially adds, "was that when I walked off after loudly repudiating the business, I found myself face to face with the bull. He had jumped the fence and was charging down the passage on the other side of the *barrera*. He looked me in the eye and I looked him in the eye. We called it quits. It didn't take me long to climb the footholds on the wall up into the lower tier of seats. My story was that I was finding an elevated spot to make sketches from." What enabled him to stand "the American part of the crowd" was "the young woman along," discreetly unnamed. "We built ourselves a sort of private box from which we looked out at these goings on, in them but not of them," he writes, as if setting up *U.S.A.*'s Camera Eye.

They were not, as Stewart assumed, making love in the room he gave up to Crys, although they discussed sex and marriage, Dos saying that while not intrinsically beautiful, these were "the only thing on earth that opens doors instead of closing them." The nervous and naive young man and woman agreed that children were too important to miss. When writing for the theater in Paris at the war's end Dos had been drawn to handsome, lively Kate Drain, the nurse's aide who married his friend John Howard Lawson. In the twenties Lawson wrote left-wing dramas alongside Dos; in the thirties he was a stalwart of the Popular Front and was later pegged as one of the Hollywood Ten. Dos was close to the couple and their child, Alan, in New York, and his response to their rocky marriage—they divorced in '23—fed the plot of *Manhattan Transfer*. But it was Crystal who deeply stirred him. She was "the first and only person he had felt permanent about," he said. Responsive as she was to men's personalities and to their drive, he was the first she "could think of marrying." In *The Best Times* their interlude in Pamplona shows the truth of Ben Franklin's saying, "A man and a woman are like a pair of scissors. Neither one is any good without the other." On a day trip to San Sebastian on the coast Dos urged Crys to get married then and there. Each would have moments of wishing they had.

Saying no but willing to be engaged, she couldn't realize how hard it would be for a writer without money or family to follow through on this lofty state with no encouragement from her family. Although Dos was not her first ardent suitor, she had no idea how fiercely her father would object, believing she could bring the men together. She'd write home from Strasbourg that she was "pretty much in love but calmly, and considering the idea of marriage with a certain person," finding the process "not romantic but deadly real." She confessed to having "lots of girlish folderol inside me about the finality of forsaking all others for a mere human being—me in my glory and every day up for a three-cylinder model." Dos said he had "five out of a possible four" cylinders (he would joke that FDR's New Deal reforms should include the forty-eight-hour day). She told him she belonged as much to the home folks as to herself, that they had a right to demand the ceremonial trappings when she married. She wanted to have it both ways—to give her family a wedding while choosing her own husband. She thought she could square the circle.

They separated at the end of the festival. With summer passing, Crystal was determined to begin work on her thesis in Strasbourg, while after these emotionally charged weeks Dos needed a long walk through the Pyrenees into France, in their "silence and solitude" a magnet to him amid the "gabblegabble" around the tables under the portales at Pamplona. He was ready for high trails where scenery unrolled "on either side like the painted panorama they used to unroll during the Rhine music in Siegfried." Crystal knew she couldn't keep up, but he recruited three companions (one dropped out along the way) including Chink Dorman-Smith, a British officer who was the Hemingways' close friend and turned out to be "just the kind of reliable man you would want to climb a mountain with." Hemingway stayed behind, worried by Hadley's late period, according to Reynolds, though Dos says they left him happily fishing in the next valley. He was not in as good physical shape as Dos Passos, and whenever Hem's name came up Chink remarked "he was a likely lad," always in the past tense, to Dos a joke, though hearing it would make Hadley nervous, as if she could foresee the change Pauline Pfeiffer's entry into their ménage the next year brought in her husband.

Dos sent notes to Crys as the thirteen-day hike stretched out, "stony paths up to such passes as you dream of where one loses the way and scrambles about fighting one's knapsack." The Valle de Ordesa, below Mont Perdu, was "a grassy bottom with a stream in it, fringed with pinewoods and hemmed in by tremendous brick and slate-colored walls and bastions. There's no town in it, no shepherds, nothing but two little white inns, extraordinarily clean and well cared for. The afternoon is spent basking in idleness and eating of wild strawberries. This walk's one of the best ever, perhaps the best ever." Crystal, now reading Havelock Ellis's *The Soul of Spain*, was prepared to be told, "You've got to come here that's all there is about it." When urging him to visit her in Strasbourg, she had invoked "the plaid gods of maidens who roam amidst desolate mediocrity," and he now complained that her maidenly self stood in their way: "Why in the name of the Eleven Thousand Virgins who were drowned in the Rhine aren't you here? It's too annoying. Love Dos." Into another note he tucked a spring of "edelweiss captured most dangerously shinnying up a rock flue on Mont Perdu." When it was over, he recounted the hike, the Spanish countryside and people, in a 1,500-word letter imbued with his delight in the experience. It belongs in an anthology of twentieth-century American prose:

> *Hôtel du Cap*
> *Antibes*
> *Alpes Maritimes*
>
> We left Burguete one fine morning, Chink George Mac and I with Hem to put us on our road into the next valley where he was going to fish. Splendid misty morning through wooded ridges and then down

into a deep gorge where was the town of Arive. Then we drank a sort of stirrup cup of coffee and the expedition started up the hill toward the next ridge at a good clip leaving Hem to his gorge and his trout. Up through pleasant villages and then up a zigzag mulepath where we sweated our first agonized climbing sweat to a splendid town named Aldaurrea Alta from which you could see green and blue and purple ridges in every direction and a patch of snow eastward among the clouds. Finest old redfaced people in the town and cold sweet water in the fountain. Then through pinewoods to a place bearing the fairground name of Jaurietta where we lunched off red wine and omelets and Chink tried to explain to the *carabinieros* that they ought to use skis in winter. Rather full of food we staggered down from *Jaurietta* into the *Valle de Salazar* and found ourselves at nightfall in a little place called *Fuesa* where there was no inn and it looked for a while as if we were going to have to sleep on the side of the road. Eventually the people who kept the main store took us in very kindly & gave us food and beds in which we slept like rocks.

Next day we walked with the postman, a stumpy bandylegged man with a large nose who walks incredibly fast, to a town called Garde where the church had a superb Chirrigueresque altablo crowded with [*gaudines*] like the end of the first act at the Ziegfeld follies. From there we crossed a high wild pass with considerable losing of the path and stumbling among the underbrush to Anso. Anso is an amazing place in upper Aragon. People still wear the old Aragonese costumes, broad black felt hats and knee britches and different colored dresses for married and unmarried women and/or widows. Had a peculiarly fine swim in the river below the town. Anso is a place to go to.

The following day was hair-raising, we went over high passes, got lost a great many times. Met some fine people in a field way up in a pass before *Aragues del Puerto* who told us not to worry if we [were] getting away from the police that the people in the mountains would help us every time. After lunch while bathing my feet in the river under a poplar tree I had a long interview with a rather irritated *carabinieri* who could not read my passport and insisted I had come from France. He finally left me with a parting shot that he couldn't understand my Spanish anyway so it was no use talking. To which I gleefully assented. He was the only unpleasant person we met on the whole trip. We finally crawled into a place named *Castillo de Jaca* in pitch darkness walking on our hands and knees from exhaustion. There were no beds in the *posada* so we happily went to sleep in the straw in the barn.

The next day was not too long and extraordinarily pleasant. We lunched and laid up for the heat of the day under a walnut tree in the garden of Larosa. The man and his wife who ran the posada were very courtly and fed us most handsomely. We crossed a couple of fine passes in the afternoon and arrived in *Biescas* in a state of decent preservation. In *Biescas* Mac left us by bus for France having suddenly remembered engagements in Paris. We talked there to a returned soldier who had been 18 months prisoner of the Moors of the Riff shut up in a quarry underground. He was our Enoch Arden. As we sat drinking coffee outside the fonda waiting for the bus that was taking Mac to some little village where his family lived, some girls he knew passed without recognizing him.

From *Biescas* a supremely fine walk took us over the Cuello del *Cotefablo* to *Bosto,* a most fantastic town in a roaring gorge where we arrived late at night stumbling along the stoney pass. All that day's villages were notable, *Yesios, Finas, Foangie.* In *Bosto* the first great battle with bedbugs took place. Chink was spurred to it not so much by the pain of the bites as by moral indignation at the idea that such there should be in a world where Britannia ruled the waves. I caused great scandal by sleeping through unbitten in a room off a little balcony full of white pigeons. From *Bosto* we walked up the canyon to the *Valle d'Vodeva* a wild valley hemmed in by tier after tier of cliffs that guard the back of *Mont Perdu.* We did only three hours to an inexpensive but clean and most pleasant mountain inn run by some Alpine club or other. Lucky that we found it because it rained all afternoon.

The next morning with a guide and mist-hampered-by-Alpine view & the fact that the sky looked like rain we set out to cross the *Col du Gaulis* and then on over the mountains into the *Valle de Bielsa*. The guide led us over Col du Gaulis alright and a fine walk it was—but then we got to scrambling along ledges and cliffs above and wild valleys below until at last we got to a corner where the guide threw in the sponge and admitted he knew no more about the path than we did. Followed a lively two hours. It was wonderful such scrambling along ledges of crumbling shale, such handing up of packs and sticks and the guide's little dog, such passionate embracing of smooth white rock as you never did see. The guide's last injunction was—If you find yourself falling, take off your shoes [Dos draws this on the margin]. It was much appreciated. At last we found ourselves on the edge of a razorback pass. The guide pointed vaguely down into the valley that we overhung and said our road lay below us, which it did, very far below, explained that his father would be worried about him and left us. We ate chocolate and rested and eventually, I don't know exactly how, got down into that valley bottom, most by sliding on our tails on the crumbling shale, and about midnight staggered into *Biesca* having walked about 14 hours straight.

Next day a rather easy walk through more inconceivable gorges and over a path full of springs brought us to *Benasque* an ancient lost town with a fine old *fonda* in antique style and a church full of bits of Romanesque sculpture. From Benasque another tremendous walk with a good path took us over the pass into France. That next day we spent collecting some money for George and then whisked over another pass into the *Val d'Avon*. Next day mostly by road over the *de la Buraigo* to *Estavar,* a thoroughly *Catalan* town full of the usual rumors of revolution in Barcelona. In *Flavorsi* we found a fiesta going on and an inn full of jollification and a brass band. It was one jumping-off place for *Andorra*.

In the company of a little boy from Barcelona who was also *de excursio•*, we walked up the valley in the morning to a place called *Tor*. There's no describing the road to *Tor*, the sort of dizzy path you go along in dreams sometimes. In *Tor* we had the meal of the whole trip, tostilla and ham and potatoes and honey and delicious black wine. Everything unbelievably good, served us by a woman with a sharply cut transparent gaunt face that might have been made out of the very white pentelic marble, who spoke a caressing dialect of *langue d'oc* probably the very language of Vidal and [?]. I'd like to have stayed for weeks in *Tor*. Then began one of our fantastic afternoons, lost the road, the little Barcelona boy, lost each other and ourselves until at last we found ourselves rolling down a vast grassy slope into a blue tangle of valleys that a man said was *Andorra*. We shot into *Andorra* like out of a gun, I vowing and protesting that I wanted to stop in the villages, and after a *haute Romanesque* scramble down a pitch black gorge in a thunderstorm we arrived, streaming water, howling for food at a dilapidated inn in a town that we could hear by the great roar of its water spouts rather than see, meat for the bedbugs of the Capital. Here in *Antibes* I'm resting easily in a large empty hotel of faintly decaying splendor with the Murphys and Don Stewart. Thanks so much for sending my suit down. I arrived in a state of odorous dilapidation unbelievable to beholders.

Write me here. (It's definitely not *du Pape*.)

Hemingway would boast his friends walked 4,169 kilometers in fourteen days. Returning to Paris, Crys carried with her Don Stewart's laundry, consisting of socks and underclothes, with some films of Georgia O'Keeffe they wanted taken across the border and Hemingway's library books, which she returned to Sylvia Beach, reporting on the Pamplona fiesta. Sylvia—whom Crystal much admired—must have been delighted to hear of Dos's determined letter, for she esteemed his physical energy as well as his mind. After a second night in Paris, Crys caught the train back to Strasbourg, and in her nest there wrote home speculating what sort of husband Dos might be. A bohemian always on the move, he would be difficult for the Rosses to absorb, she told her family, and if she married him, she would "never have peace or cottonwool domesticity." On the other hand, she'd "have other things and always more of you than by a more conventional marriage. I feel as if I have bumped into my destiny," she said, "but I mean to be deadly sure." There were things they wanted to do together in Europe, and if indeed she loved him, it would be practical to marry, in which case they might do so secretly, she suggested, a flight of fancy she immediately regretted since it would worry her people and put Dos, who'd said nothing of the sort, in the wrong. She made clear her loyalty and determination "to finish this embryonic doctorate." Financially dependent on the Rosses for the time being—the scholarship was for the first year of her studies, and about to run out—she would afterward earn money and always "under my own name, C. R. R." Dashing all this off, she went to bed, resolved to attack her thesis in the morning.

On August 1—not long before Dos was scheduled to visit Strasbourg—came a cable from Dr. Ross, "FOR GOD'S SAKE WAIT TODAY'S LETTER." Replying reassuringly, she read over the [blue] carbon of her letter to them. On the back she noted in hand: "All this, an absurd preparedness program—blue poppycock. Mother & Dad—I want to do right by them, consideration their due tho prowling strangers break into our circle—foreordained the question, how happiest? But I am an insolent creature—bay at moon—barking at sun I can break a circle & preserve it intact even tighter. Love & duty are appalling. I am 24—Crystal R."

Love and Duty

CRYSTAL'S FAITH IN THE power of her will was variously challenged during her long life, and the self-confidence she brought to love and duty could not have survived her father's letter. He condescends to his "Dear Baby Girl," saying, "You're merely infatuated by the glamour of the thing, the fact that he won a little distinction one time or was mentioned as a heavyweight in modern literature some years ago, and now you are run off or out of your head and flattered into thinking you are in love with him." There are three thousand such words of warning: Marriage in France was a Catholic ceremony [it wasn't]. Dos Passos was a Catholic [he wasn't] and would have to bring up his children in the church. Dos is derided as a penniless Mexican ("Shun Dos Pessos [*sic*] as you would a viper"), Crystal told she shamed her father with his fellow Masons [he was a future head of the Grand Lodge of Texas]. Doctor Ross was more than a doting, sentimental, overconcerned father, if not necessarily the villain he may here appear. His histrionic tendency blinded him to the strength of character he had fostered in this daughter. Claiming to have aged five years while writing these pages, he wallows in a Victorian version of Lear on the heath as he closes:

I am trying hard to be brave and through hope and through Faith,
to believe that you will not fail me, AND IF YOU DO [capitalization
his] THEN THE STARS HAVE GONE OUT OF MY HEAVENS AND
ONLY GOD IS MERCIFUL BUT NATURE HAS FAILED ME,
AND MY FATHERHOOD IS A BLUR AND A BYWORD AND A
JEST AND ALL A HIDEOUS NIGHTMARE.

    With all my love I am DADDY.

Doctor Ross's Cordelia replied to this delusional cri de coeur in tactful and loving pages addressed to her "Dears": "Infatuation?—no—not for even thirty minutes. Ask Dos. But I have hoped that when life beckoned I'd get up and follow the call. I know quite well one leaves soft warm things behind. I have always wanted to keep mounting up all my life, never to arrive on a plateau of development, no matter how pleasant the plateau might be, and I think marrying an individual of Dos's character, or not marrying at all, is the way." Her speculation about a secret marriage has made the situation harder for them and for Dos Passos, but no lasting harm is done: "I do not think you made a mess of raising me because I was honest enough to meet a vital question vitally and immediately—without all the customary paraphernalia of subterfuge and gradual approach. I never met but one man I could think of marrying and when I did I told you about it that is all." Crystal would hold to her credo and the acerb belief in individual integrity that backed it. But it was easier to be firm on paper than in person, and she gravely underestimated her father's righteous patriarchal instinct. In her next letter home she is "being convinced very gradually and quietly, that I am perhaps soberly in love with this absurd Dos and that my life will probably be richer with him than without him." She includes one of his notes about the walking trip through "the heart of a wild savage amiable country—little valleys he says perched on dizzy mountains where the people are nice clean and simple." Her father is ostensibly satisfied, cabling "WELL HAPPY TRUSTING. DADDY." But his suspicions are not assuaged, and she says she won't marry until back from France. "Given a thesis just begun and terribly difficult," she would consider taking Dos Passos to Texas and returning to Strasbourg to do the dissertation, but thinks it not "fair to the man to trot home thousands of miles with a suitor to whom one is not married." She backs away from confrontation and doesn't confide in Dos about what she calls the "insurmountable difficulties" ahead of them.

From Antibes he replies to a chatty note written when Madame Epp had tucked her into bed after a frustrating day on the thesis: "I'm still resting in the luxurious laps of Gerald and Sara Murphy swimming morning, noon and night, etc. I think I'll make an offensive in the direction of Strasbourg at the end of the week. This is Monday so furbish up your chainmail and be ready." Though he tries to be amusing in his desire for her, Dos pushed hard and, being a gentleman, kept urging her to get married. She had much to show him in her little city, yet the visit was stressful enough that, back in Paris, he halfway apologizes: "I'm a goddamned idiot—forgive me—I'll be more sensible, less sensible, another time. I was in a sort of daze, and the last half hour with you sprang the trap. I'm made like that, that's all, now to collect moneys for London." He had asked her to accompany him on a visit to the courtesy aunts in Kew who took care of him as a child, Auntie Kate [Gee] and Auntie Lou [Meakin]. Crystal told her family she'd refuse, but a card from him written at a café evidently changed her mind: "There are formations in the marble of this table top like the tales and rumps of white horses wonderfully in relief," he noted. "Good God, we mustn't pass up anything." He had first to find the cash:

> Crys: This is how it is so far, no news of any sort from my aunt. I can't imagine what has happened to her or the family fortunes. I've wired Brandt to try to get an advance from my publisher so there's nothing to do but sit pretty. A good chance to do a great deal of consequitive/consecutive (how do you spell it?) work as I don't know anybody here except the Hemingways and will have no money for distractions. The Hems look fine and were so pleased

to hear about the baby. Hadley said you told her everything she needed to know about it.

Look Crys we must see each other again before I go back to America. Toodledoo the little dog belonging to my little old ladies in Kew is dead and they have gone to the country for two weeks—so I have plenty of time to get to London. If we can't make it England, we can make it somewhere nearer. The main result of coming down here was to find great gobs of miscellaneous mail that needs answering. So here I am *au quatriéme* [in the quarter] at the *Hôtel du Pavillon* and it's raining and I'm trying to get rid of seven million letters before starting a novel.

Go and drink some *vin chaud* for me. Write me here at the hotel 6 *rue du Verneuil*. Be good to yourself Crys. Love Dos.

A second note says the Protectoress on Riverside Drive has sent no money: "Hello Crys, The Financial Situation is still strange, but immediate improvement is promised by letter. Also 300 dollars now at large somewhere in Europe—so by the middle of next week I may be wealthy and *disponible* [able to be moved about like troops]—But I'll write." Along with her loyalty to her family and the emotional baggage he carried from his, Dos's poverty shaped their relations. He had given a power of attorney to Aunt Mamie when he came back from the Ambulance Service and joined the Medical Corps in 1918. Though he loved the farm on the Potomac as his father had, he wanted nothing to do with inherited property and didn't look into her stewardship for two decades, during which, according to Ludington, "Mr. Gordon and his son-in-law Byron Ralston collected income from the land amounting to approximately $100,000, only $15,000 of which was ever turned over to Dos Passos." Several thousand a year would have changed life for the artist who had regularly to ask for cash and visit pawn shops when it didn't arrive, enjoying creature comforts he'd grown up with only on visits to friends like the Murphys. In *Dos Passos: A Life,* Carr shows that two money-raising contracts on the house and land were later put through and Dos told nothing. James R. Gordon—whom Crystal once talked with on the phone, remembering him as "bristling"—and his son-in-law (the Ralstons owned the apartment on Riverside Drive) were at best incompetent stewards. This darkened Dos's vision beginning with *Three Soldiers,* in novels where capitalism threatens every prospect of personal happiness. The young writer's politics marked for Wilson "some stubborn sentimentalism of which his misapplied resentments represent the aggressive side," and in a review of 1929, the same year as the portrait of Hugo in *I Thought of Daisy,* Wilson foresaw the redirection of Dos's anarchistic radicalism against the Left after the Soviet Union's NKVD (People's Commissariat for Internal Affairs) had Robles killed. This registered in his New Deal trilogy, *District of Columbia,* and when he sued to recover his Virginia property during World War II.

From Paris he resumed the bulletins to Crystal:

> For the moment, I'm being fed and chatted by the Hemingways.
> It's a rainy afternoon. I'm trying to write a big scene in a roadhouse
> but I'm not getting ahead very much. Paris is anodyne, dense with its
> usual mistily sensual melancholy.
> Love, Dos

His sensibility in these letters—these moments of reaching out, the opening up of the heart—are what drives and will drive his fiction.

> Went to the *Monte de Piété* to hock my typewriter. There was an old
> woman with those little ostrich plumes, a terrible wreck of a woman.
> They wouldn't give her anything on them. You can't imagine how
> they trembled in her swollen hands when she picked them off the
> counter saying, *"Ah ça s'abime si vite"* [One forgets things so quickly].
> I'm on the trail of my finances and by next week expect to be
> rolling in gold: *Si on pouvrait combiner quelque chose* [if one could
> combine certain things].

Blessed as it is by love of her, his desire is fierce:

> Crys: It will be the death of Hubsch [her dance partner poet] but
> either I shall come back to Alsace very soon, or we shall both go to
> some convenient Jericho or I shall blow up and bust. It's a rotten
> shame and there's nothing to be done about it but hang round
> you some more. So you're warned now. The whistle has blown. *Sauve
> qui peut* [every man for himself].
>
> A first advent of relief in the shape of 780 francs from the
> *TransAtlantic Review* makes me feel my oats kind of [Ford was
> paying his contributors]. I must wait until the famous 300 is sighted.
> Then you just watch out, little Red Riding Hood, cause the Wolf is
> after you. The better to see the better to hear you the better to eat
> you little girl.

What she had said of Brother's protective stance rankled with Dos.
"And after all, no harm comes to good little girls," he mocks. "Their
brothers come and rip open the wolf's belly and there she is inside
little Red Riding Hood and all." He closes, "I want you so Crys." A
discouraged postcard follows: "I'd love to hear from you sometime if
you feel like it. You know one can be too hard on people, it's all such
a toss up—but just as you like—Love Dos." The money comes through
from a publisher, and their trip is on:

> The Brandts have sent me $300 extracted somehow from Doran—
> so the Privy Purse is again fat. Here's 500 francs I owe you. $200 for
> the Esterri money [which she had sent to him in Spain] $300 for the
> [unclear] $20—deducting divers monies spent on you.
>
> Look Crys, where do you want to go and when? I want to be in
> London in about 10 days when my little old ladies will be back from
> their 2 weeks in the country. We can't be too long in England as
> it's very expensive. Would you like to take any sort of intermediate
> trip? We could go to Brussels or the Channel Islands. It'll be raining

everywhere so it's much the same. If you haven't any spot cash money I can divvy up my three hundred. What do you think? Look on your map and write me. It'd only cost 50 francs for me to come up to Strasbourg to fetch you. Or I could meet you in Brussels.

A society of yodelers possibly Tyrolean is passing under the window. *Extraordinaire.* [I'll wait] for a letter or a telephone. It won't hurt me to finish my roadhouse scene.

Love Dos

One goes to the Channel Islands by boat from *St. Malo* in Normandy. And other boats take one to England therefrom. If I don't hear I shall appear beating and tootleing a one man band along the *Quai St. Thomas* to the grand scandal of the concierges, so look out.

It's now making a great thunderstorm out—superb. The Tyroleans are still yodeling dimly in the little bistro *rue Verneuil*—Jesus you ought to see it rain.

She loved visiting the ladies with whom he had been parked off and on from the ages of six to ten when his mother accompanied his father on business trips in Europe or the States. They called Dos "Jack" and liked her. When they showed him a magnificent highboy that was his parents', and he had it put out on the street, she saw something in Dos of the generation of Max Eastman and Mabel Dodge, the latter of whom spoke of "the pleasure of seeing old fussy things blown up." As a literary modernist, he took with him to New York two sacred texts, Joyce's *Ulysses* from Sylvia Beach's shop and the expanded *In Our Time,* which Hemingway's friends were promoting with publishers.

From London they caught a boat to Bruges, whence she could return to Strasbourg by train. Agreeing to renounce "a honeymoon in Holland," they took a walk as far as the Dutch city of Delft. He would allude to the missed opportunity in a letter from Manhattan that closes, "Don't forget to find out if eggs are always cold for breakfast in Rotterdam," and she acknowledged receipt of "two dishes of cold boiled potatoes," endowing them with the taste of [illegible]. On their last night together she wanted "to give him more intimacy." Before he left her at the Maritime Terminus Hotel, she accepted from Dos a large emerald that had been his father's, which in Strasbourg they'd had set into a ring, signifying they would marry.

As a critical year for them began he sent a card from London, where he caught the train to Southampton, then the ferry to Le Havre and a liner to New York:

> Gosh Crys I haven't mailed Madame's letter yet. I just found it. I'll send it off immediately. You should have seen the Great Caruso. He looked rather like a barber, a super barber. How was the Maritime Terminus?
>
> This is Monday and I'm off tonight for *Havre*. Your flowers were very appreciated at Kew. Be most especially good to yourself.

A note from the French port conveys a completion of sorts:

> Found your Maritime Terminus letter Crys. I was eaten by fleas coming over on the boat from Southampton. I have all of the gray restless day to spend here before the boat leaves. I shall sit in empty cafes drinking and plotting devilment apocrypha in the company of blue siphons and unsatisfactory chairs.
>
> I'm looking forward to the [illegible]. This Terminus is not worthy of the exalted name. *Havre* though gray and scruffy seems sunlight and the pomp of Nineveh after England. But I must go and walk about. I still feel as if you were with me. Love Dos.

PART II

Winter Struggles, Spring Blues

CRYSTAL WOULD REMAIN PROUD of having shared in the making of wine from grapes in France that October. On the train back from Brussels, enjoying the company of a Spanish woman dancer, she was glad to find that the leaves hadn't turned, and from Strasbourg rushed out to the village of Riquewihr. Evoking possible futures, she reported to Dos, "I shall live there three months someday if my third son has brown eyes or if the university gives me a leave of absence." Old Europe's *vendange* beguiled the citizen of a land locked in Prohibition:

You stand and you stoop, working along a row but altogether— singing and from time to time someone screams Foool! Meaning Full, and the amiable idiot George comes up with a [drawing] this shape on his back and empties the wooden can. Foool—that's the chorus. Try it Dos.

Shriek every ten minutes or so for relief, "Idiot"—like a song—in 26 voices *ici, là bas* [here, there], sort of yodeled. The streets are running with new wine now, and they dump the pressed mess into the 700-year-old bring-your-own-kodak wells. These containers [she draws one] line the lanes and the streets, even the *rue de la Couronne*,

filled with crushed squished putrifying amber and red grapes.
The modest proprietors discourage flies with a covering of
leaves. The wine I had trickling out of the press. No wonder about
anything anymore, that is, anything cool.

"It was gorgeous," she says: "Best [time] I've had," but "I had to leave
the sun-mist slope even—saved for the last—and do conferences."

She had let him think she was further along with O. Henry and
Maupassant than she was, for a letter from New York that crossed with
this begins: "How's Strasbourg? I suppose you are having to defend
your thesis now. More power to you!" Dos no longer judges the city
bad for writers:

> New York is superb. O Crys you ought to see the weather—day after
> day sunny and autumnal ripe with an occasional cold wind to let you
> know winter's coming. I'm in a rather pleasant room at 11 Bank
> Street for the moment. It has a gas burner that I cook coffee and
> toast on for [breakfast?] and a picture of Woodrow Wilson that I find
> staring spitefully at me when I wake up in the morning. The book
> publishing censorship gets worse and worse. I'm afraid I'll soon have
> to take to some honest method of earning my living.
>
> Did you get the $100? Of course I landed just before Columbus Day
> so it was the 15th before I could get the money sent off. Hope it didn't
> put you out. I'm ensconced in work except for an occasional party or
> bad gin and worse wine. My play has gone all fluey. The people got
> cold feet and couldn't raise the money or something.

Like more than one solitary stylist from James through Mailer, Dos
Passos yearned for success in the theater's collaborative art. One reason
he "didn't sleep in that other bed at the Terminus Maritime," a later
letter tells Crystal, was the "accursed play" he'd felt he must finish in
New York, an expressionistic drama called *The Moon and a Gong*, re-
named *The Garbage Man* and produced with Dos's sets in Cambridge

in May 1925. Like "July," it was a section of "Work in Progress." "Talk about remorse," he recalled of saying goodbye to her in Holland, "It's the things you leave undone that torture you, not the things you do."

She acknowledged receipt of the cold potatoes and of "ninety-nine dollars via the Bankers Trust Company and one monsieur Crystal Ross, whom the Societie of Alsace and Lorraine doubted even in my girlish presence." She asked, "What's superb about New York?"—she would one day be a New Yorker—adding, "I sort of need to know. The need is not immediate." Dos said the weather was wonderful—he'd taken a hike in Westchester County and "even that most jejeune of landscapes had considerable life to it." Two weeks later he reported: "New York is amazingly fine this autumn. More of the splendor that was Rome and the etc. that was Greece than ever." The theater was "pretty insipid," the literati "emotic," but "the yellow lights on Fifth Avenue on account of it's being a hundred years old rather make up for it." He had to make headway with *Manhattan Transfer,* as he was moving from this room, where he could hear barges on the river, to one in Brooklyn Heights with a grand view of New York harbor and wondering how to afford the thirty-five dollars per month. Urging her to be good to herself, he added, "Have just finished reading *Beyond the Pleasure Principle,* quite the most heart rending of Mr. F's books."

Crystal returned from Riquewihr to the thesis struggle. O. Henry, who died in 1911, had acknowledged Maupassant's influence, flattered when likened to him, and she had signed on for the comparison. She found no significant relationship but couldn't "cut and run," regretting this in the letter to her brother that also recants her talk of a secret marriage. Touched by the Whitman of "The Open Road" and "Out of the Cradle," the Melville of *Moby Dick,* the young woman for whom Paris was "a great golden sweep" and Strasbourg deeply charming submerged herself in the colorist's anecdotes of the South and West and of Broadway. "I tried to say that his cowboys talk like intoxicated dictionaries," she wrote to Dos, that "the Negro minstrels and advance agents for a minstrel show melanged, and I succeeded in saying that his diction is sometimes over-colored." She could work up the backdrop of Poe, Hawthorne, and the American short story, and enjoyed assessing O. Henry personally, but she had no idea how to relate his writings to the ironical Frenchman's.

At her typewriter around the clock for a month, she produced a draft that seemed between M.A. and Ph.D. length and handed it in to a placidly nice professor whose competence she doubted. Commenting admiringly, he shared it with a Polish colleague whom she thought intelligent and feared, not surprised to hear that the man was prejudiced against comparative literature. "They never had a doctorate here before and are stalled for a precedent. To make one of me would certainly be an academic catastrophe," she told Dos. While waiting on "these professors" she put in weeks on the language she likened to "water charged with chlorine" and to "delicate crystal—a fluid glass." Crystal's French is not only grammatically correct but sophisticated in diction. It was fun to share the language with someone who could use it, and the letters to Dos can fall into *franglais:*

Dos, my extreme darling it is twenty minutes after eleven on the morning of Saturday, the eighth of November. The housework is finished, the flowers are all freshened and arranged. Our mother in Wissenbourg sent us a basket of *legumes* [vegetables]—darn I can't smoke and play on little Alonzo Remington's piazza *à la foi* [at the same time]—wait a minute. Everything is so sweet and the brussel sprouts bubbling on the stove keep sending insistent tendrils of *odeur* down the dark channel flanked with irritating *armoires* [bureaus]—O wait a minute—so I thought the thing needing *fuming* [smoking] up a bit. Madame urges all men to smoke all the time but thinks women injure possible children. What with swimming and dancing and *couring* [running] about bare-headed, I have murdered all mine. It's a pity too because they were going to have such beautiful bodies and brown eyes—that may be why you were born. O heck, I'll just chew the tobacco—the smoke gets in my eyes.

She calls her typewriter Alonzo for her father but wants to have brown-eyed Dos's children, which may now seem unlikely. No longer burning the candle with parties and booze, she chases "the gorgeous lilting sun" with her table and chair all over her room at 3 Quai St. Thomas: "I taste the sun and lick it like an all day sucker these days, because we do become the land of dead all-day-long dusks," she writes. She brings democratic instincts to a high bourgeois household. From childhood close to her family's Negro housekeeper, Ava, Crys tells Dos that "in our darkest days of Southern slavery we never approached the *esclavage* that Madame Epp and her kind inflict on their servants." Their "*mélange* [mixture] of *gentillesse* and *petitesse* [her word for pettiness]" makes her "so blooming mad":

> An intelligent woman, far more capable [than her mistress] by right of execution and endless back-breaking, [Marie] has to ask her dame's permission to run to the corner and buy a spool of thread, and then Madame deducts 10 francs from the wage for *caisse de maladie* [sick leave] or something just as absurd and feels like a queen who stoops to be noble when she drags the poor girl out to the cinema, the cinema she chooses. Marie thrilled me when she said she'd just as leave walk to the *cinema* and return with an *armoire* [chest of drawers] or a lacquered chair as with Madame.

She evokes a house where the maid lacks the nerve to leave her mistress and pretends to be sick, while the mistress does half her work and the American boarder the errands. Yet Madame Epp had saving graces. Overweight and awkward, she was courageous on a country walk. Their neighbor across the street, a charming old lady who had "white curly hair and little round red chocolate drops in her *petit ridicule* [reticule]" could cheer her up by recalling her youthful heyday, when she was "brilliant, almost beautiful, unfailingly gay." At one point the two ladies "got on the subject of her son"—he "was killed in 1915, twenty-three he was"—and Madame Epp was ashamed of what she had become. Her hate for the Germans, she confessed to her American guest, was "almost a curse."

The household drama was enlivened and the boarder happily distracted by the addition of one Constantin Cantacuzino. To her several correspondents she wrote that they were "taking another pension-naire," an event that turned out to be "too funny and after all most agreeable all round":

> There is a little Rumanian prince, 19, whose family are parking him
> to study law two years and have sought a place *assez convenable*
> [sufficiently convenient] for him to live, money no object. Prince
> Michel his father brings him. The kid wanted to go to Paris—is very
> handsome and reputed irresistible to the ladies—and the family are
> going to encase him, but he must not know it. Madame is ceding her
> *chambre*. She has changed the *armoires* and bought things for the
> toilette and crowded herself into that little dressing room until I
> shall leave. And everything is ready. Only the parents want the boy to
> seem to choose his pension himself, so it is not final. You can imagine
> how that and the fact that Jean Epp did not write for a week has
> upset us. Monday or Tuesday will tell the tale.

A later passage to Dos—headed "Unity coherence and emphasis: my room is warm"—heralds Constantin's arrival. "The prince and his father came, so I put on my jade earrings. With my presently ragged hair, they are awful," she says, but the young man is "a joy":

> He is six feet and several inches, beautiful of line and head and
> charming, just charming, princeling or otherling. Madame's
> preparations were laughable and disgusting. Her reception was
> worse, but little did he wot or has he wotted. And the cycle: he is
> late or early with unerring regularity. He takes a douche hot each
> morning and a bath when he is cold. I have never dared invade
> the bathroom, which I have regarded as a rhetorical argument for

sanitation. He floods the corridor, leaves all the doors ajar, and protests when his room smells of the *cuisine.* He sleeps until 1 on Sundays and presents himself—*avec* [having asked] *permission*—in *pongée* [silk] pajamas with a black net sheik-thing about his head. He is so beautiful I cannot eat and he tells Madame naughty stories that she says, "*heureusement* [happily]" I cannot understand and he and I both know that I don't miss a nuance. A loveable youngster and amazingly intelligent. He is 20 and *il porte plus* [seems older] especially when smoking, but he grins like 14 and has a normal appetite for Colette or Ninette and Madame de So and So.

We've had such funny scenes.

The new boarder's attentions are not a burden as those of Hessell had been and of Hubsch became. "Even Madame" sees she isn't flirting, she assures Dos.

He would rather have heard of progress on the thesis than of the princeling, for he wanted her by his side. Lockhart also expected her home. In the summer she had informed her family she might be done by Christmas, and well after she admitted being stuck in Strasbourg her mother went about "with the radiant assurance that I'm planning to surprise them." Her father spoke of paying her way to and from Texas for the holidays. Doctor Ross offered to support her through what turned out to be a second year on the *doctorat,* and when he helped arrange an invitation to teach summer school in '25, she signed the contract, thinking she had time to finish and be reunited with Dos Passos first. Immediately she doubted this. She wrote to Dos that on the night the placid young professor predictably gave in to his Polish colleague, dooming her to more miserable months, then "begged me sincerely to sleep well all the same," she was about to burst into tears on the way home, "but a man I passed said '*pauvre petite*' [poor little one] and that was too funny, and the sun did a sort of flicker through the cathedral, and my sobs were mostly dry ones." As the novelist settled into "an extraordinary fine room on Columbia Heights in Brooklyn, with all the harbor and Brooklyn Bridge spread out under my windows, and the boats that go by . . . mooing in droves like cows being driven home"— a good omen for *Manhattan Transfer*'s intertwined tales—Crystal found life "unbelievably short," and so "unsatisfactory *tout en étant* [in being] too concentrated and rich and bubbly for comprehension." Unable to reconcile love and duty via this academic exercise, she was subject to what she saw as woman's diffusion. "Do you suppose Dos, that my sweet bye and bye of being even with the world will ever be?" she wondered, hopefully adding, "You have rushed me toward it."

For Christmas her family sent a box—"fruit cake and sugared pecans and little fruit fig hope balls rolled in coconut and squished cookies all red & green & hollied into a lily soda cracker box and that embroidered into a tarpaulin"—that would cause her to appreciate "my Rosses" all over again when it arrived on George Washington's Birthday. A Christmas letter to Dos asks what to do about "Mickey's poems," which he had sent her when their relationship began: "Ask the *Imprimerie Strasbourgeoise* about them, or just make a careful nice copy for his mother myself and bind it?" She looks back on her friendship with McCormick in Austin: "Mickey and I used to go down, via Mary Jane [Clorinda's predecessor] and afternoons like this, have the coffee *melanged* and ground before us and then square ourselves into his little neatness to drink it. The neighbors talked and so did we. I have nothing at all to say to his mother, and I have the manuscript in my trunk." It would remain there. Dos had considered "getting 500 copies printed and sent around, but I suppose it is a rather futile idea," he wrote New Year's Eve. He'd have no authority in the literary world "until *Manhattan Transfer,* if then," and "a gorgeous view of all New York to South Ferry and a million tug boats and million barges and a million steamers moving and chugging about" failed to cheer him up. "It may be Christmas, or it may be the gas heater, or it may be *Lacrymae Rerum* or the fact that I overate terribly yesterday, but I feel very blue today, have those do nothing blues." He commiserates about the thesis: "I'd hoped you'd be all through and off to Italy or winter sports by this time. I hate to think of you wasting valuable and irretrievable hours in the terrible herbarium of scholarship." The American writers of the twenties, many from the old universities, brought British and American models to their native materials but aimed to "make it new," in Pound's words in 1912, and were skeptical of the academy. "If you really like [your subject] of course it won't be wasted time,' but 'your hard labor for the vintage is a million times worth [doing]," he writes, "You've got a lot of things on me Crys, and that certainly isn't the least of them."

Again he urges her to polish off the degree:

> Be good to yourself Crys and write what's happening about the thesis. Is it a life and works and appreciation (by one who knows) of O. Henry now? I think it's all just a plot to keep you there on the part of the Strasbourgers.
>
> My little old ladies send their love to you for Christmas and a picture, by Miss Meakin, of Vixen, the new little dog.
>
> Don't forget to find out if eggs are always cold for breakfast in Rotterdam.
>
> Love, Dos

She has had a taste of winter sports, as he'd hoped:

> The skiing—I never saw skiing at home you know, nor snow. Constantin went up to *Camp du Fichier* [yesterday]. I was still in the O'Hell [O. Henry] session so I only went this morning in those damn shoes that undid me in Spain—I was ski-less and the snow was up to my knees for an hour or so, white cold still. I thot I'd founder and stay there in spite of my energetic red petticoat. I stumbled into the cabin and fell out again skinned. Great! But when I see a bit of white gluey stuff on the pavement it reminds me of the washhouse back home and the way starch bubbles thickly on washday.

The Rumanian's presence made Dos's absence harder: "I left early because I wanted the walk thru the forest—the path isn't so difficult alone—and I was just toasting my frozen-all-day feet & saying phrases at you when Madame came in from the *cuisine* and Constantin, starved and curious to have missed me. He is adorable, and trustable enough if you don't make a point of it." Another letter declares: "We suspect Constantin of gambling. He says he has a flair. He's going to threaten his father to lend his name to the movies to get money for a little Citroen. I feel awfully old except when I dance with him."

The day arrives when she feels on top of the thesis:

> To state facts—for the last three weeks & three days I've sat at a desk (accumulating fat where I don't want it) and tried to concoct something in the *style* of O. Henry—Frenched. Then the nights I've placed my little Lonnie [close friends called Dr. Ross "Lon"] on the marble topped stove and stood in that corner Penelope-ing [doing work she will redo the next day]. God, I've slept from 2 to 2. Madame is so furious bless her blue eyes that she threatens to write my family in English. She used to get just as mad when I danced the nights out. I'll be hanging the footnotes onto the bottom of a chapter for the tall sweet prof. & then I'll be down two weeks concentrated writing for the other. If God is better than my own pushin' powers, I'll get the thing over just before or just after Easter! Isn't that abominable? I envy you, at least you're in a self-fabric. "The sailor's wife, the sailor's star shall be / Heigh ho we go, across the sea."

An ocean stretched between her and Dos, whose patience weakened as the novel ground on. He had run into Cabell Greet, deep in the manuscript of Reginald Peacock, "a fifteenth-century divine," for his Columbia dissertation: "We talked about you walking down Seventh Avenue. I declared you were the world's loveliest, most abominable, most delightful, most annoying, most surprising, startling, unpredictable etc. person. And you're all of that Crys and more." Cabell told him Crys had written "about the Rumanian." "I don't trust them," Dos kids her. "They put rose leaves in their cigarette cases." In reply, she would like to see their friend Greet "doing a divine as limited as O. Henry, and surprised to see him takin' me up on a Rumanian rhapsody." Dos reports that *Manhattan Transfer* is "getting more indecently long": "I'm afraid it's nothing but a vast inchoate mess. I wish I'd gone to sea when I was a kid and never gotten into this beastly game of exhibitionistic sublimo-rationalizing. There's a phrase worthy of fake psychiatry for you. Be good to yourself." Crystal feeds her tensions with what she grants is a certain masochism: "O Dos aren't they comical the miseries we deal ourselves? This is going into the quick—and yet you see yourself how *stark* good it is for me—with embroidered compensations. It's just that life's too short for a person to be slow. Lackadaisy—how it makes for speed."

She plans to be done by Easter, and he wants to hold up the season till he can escape with it and her. He isn't sure of her, fears luck is against him, resolves not to suffer needlessly:

Hello Crys:

I'd like to get my work done and then have it Spring and break clean out of the morose coconut shell I live in. Like the young monk of Liberia, my existence grows drearier and drearier—golly I wish I could go to Rome with you. This damn business won't be finished before June, tho', I'm afraid, and then I don't know what I'll do Crys. I suddenly thought that perhaps when you saw me again you would not like me anymore and I felt way down. Nothing seems to go very right this winter and I have a horrid feeling that when luck is against you everything goes wrong. I wish you were here.

What are you up to? Have you got that wretched doctorate yet? Shall I have to push that Rumanian into the Elbe? Hate to think of you teaching next summer. I guess I have a mania for making myself unhappy that's all. I'm going to cut it out.

She cheers him on with the novel: "I'm glad you see the last third *de ton travail* [of your task]. Let me give you the Spring, won't you? Because

I'll be there and I'll want to." That is unconvincing, and she adds: "I don't know if I can finish. It would be so much finer to blow up instead. Think of 7 million acute accents to be proofed, 5 hours public smirking in a furrin tongue and toothpaste to be packed and people back home on the Wabash [this was a song by Theodore Dreiser's brother Paul] to be remembered." His worry that she'll stop liking him reassures her, for that couldn't happen. "Why Dos if you shouldn't like me, I'll get busy and make you or console myself findin' fault with the person you do like." Another letter declares: "You have become a sort of undercurrent. What makes undercurrents keep coming? I've always wondered. But if they took themselves off to the sea, the top would fall in." In a note he momentarily outranks Doctor Ross: "If my father's daughter has something *de beau* [beautiful], *elle te le donne* [she gives it to you]." Elsewhere she assures Dos (and herself), "If I care enough about you, I will make you and Dad love each other." She adds, "The others that he loves less are more of a comfort to him. Give me time. I'll give them grandchildren!"

She was as naively sure of Dos Passos as she had been of her family after Paris and Spain. Much as he wanted her with him, he didn't yearn to marry her as she now did to marry him. And if Madame's household drama distracted her from the thesis, Dos found time that winter and spring for his friend Lawson's plays, the painting of Lawson's sister Adelaide, and for Lawson's ex-wife, Kate Drain. Lawson was a chronically unfaithful husband, and Dos told Kate of finding him in bed with another woman. Kate was pregnant, Lawson didn't want the baby, and when they divorced in 1923 Dos may have offered to marry her and be the father, Herf's gesture in *Manhattan Transfer*. After the drunken playboy Stanwood Emery sets his apartment and himself afire, leaving his actress lover pregnant, Ellen vows to "give up all this silly life and raise [the child]," and Jimmy proposes, but their marriage soon collapses. Working through his awkwardness with women via what the novelist calls this "beastly game of exhibitionistic sublimo-rationalizing," Dos sees that he and Kate wouldn't have lasted. Crystal too could feel shaky, but she was far from these bohemian relationships in her old-fashioned confidence that love conquers all.

Dear Dos, I want to talk to you—to your shadow. Everything is cascading. It's March 3. Yesterday was Texas Independence and clean sheets. It's a fun night—champagne. Two American boys drifted by to see me just when I needed them most—ha ha—I'm about to go to Greece with the tall one only he gets drunk too quick.

I'm all upset Dos, been read'n things and not sleepin'. Good night, honey. Crys
Walked to the Rhine this morning. It's lovely and slanted and there—grey with rose.

She has reworked her schedule: "I see the end of my thesis—but I'll bump into Easter holidays and have to hang over for the *soutenance* [the defense]. Heigh ho—how I'm going' to lilt out of this town—sluffin' out of the old skin. The thesis is quite good now as to French. I have to work up some serial ideas for O. Henry. He was a funny rebel, making saints out of shopgirls skeptically." Dos writes from the Cape, where he can put New York behind him:

Hello Crys: I'm living for the moment in a little shack in Provincetown on Cape Cod. Wonderful March sunny cold clear windy weather, seagulls and lighthouses. I've spent a week out here absolutely alone, and I feel fine. Gosh this winter has been flat tires and busted springs for me. I've never been so low in my life. I even got to smelling rottenly, like a canary that's molting. I've been broke and blue and in a sort of stupor. It's been a general K.O., but just the fact that I can write about it proves that I'm on the road to recovery. Forgive me for unloading on you this way. Spring is just outside the door and seagulls and motordories popping and chugging. Out of the doldrums and into the roaring forties [he has entered his fourth decade]. Of course, by the time I'm eighty and it's too late

I may know how I ought to conduct myself in the pursuit of my
"inalienable right" to life liberty and happiness. Gosh those words
have a bitter ring to us poor devils.

Look Crys, when you leave Strasbourg I'll think of you in Rome
Easter.

Lucky devil—Love Dos

She knows she won't be lucky to leave her little city of freedom and
refuge. "I do not want ever to go home—not even to New York. I do not
want to leave so much half done, half begun, half understood, glimpsed
not followed," she answers. "Curious: *The Last Days of Pompei*—of my
Pompei—I'm rushing to finish and hating what will follow." Loyalty
to her father traps her: "I don't want to return a minute but I have to
and I want it over."

"Hello Crys. It's Spring," he writes. "The tugboats on the river are
shrieking and yodeling like love-crazy cats. It's all very disturbing—and
I've got three solid months of work to do yet. What are you up to? After
Italy where? Don't forget Mexico. Are you a *docteur* yet?" She "ought to
be sitting here looking at Brooklyn Bridge and East River. Why aren't
you? Love Dos."

In a second letter he yearns for a fresh chance at their honeymoon:

It's excessively April. The elm on Orange St. has burst into leaf. The
tugboats on the river are frantic. The little dogs frolic in the back
yards under my window—even the stolid [rumble?] of trucks—and
the car barges are putting on gaudy coloring.

I'm pretty well except that my eyes are lousy—and lonely as hell.
Christ I've got those Maritime Terminus go to Rome at Easter,
grands express international blues.

Thanks for the letters that were balm after the horrid postcard
[apparently lost]. God damn it, I wish I could go with you to Rome. I
want to bust out of this morbid innerfestering literary existence if I
can for a while—I need a sabbatical year. I've done nothing but write

since 1919. I have this play and a million debts and no money, and my novel to finish so just pipe down young man pipe down.

Be good to yourself Crys and tell those professors from me to go and drown themselves in the Rhine.

Love Dos

Crys Makes a Decision—
Dos to the Rescue

AN OPERATIC CLIMAX LOOMS in her reply:

Pipe down all you want to Dos, but I'm glad you piped up! And if it's Rome you want to go to with me, [you go] because I'm not going. I decided yesterday and slept better—damn me.

I want to go, I want a rest cure and sun shining and eternity to dazzle professorial *souvenirs* [reminders] of northern mirages. It isn't that. I've done so much that my Dad has been sporting and quiet over and I'm gonna do so much to make him howl and hurt [translation: "One way or another I'm going to marry this man and my father won't be happy"] that I haven't the courage to take his ready money and go on another month Cook's touring when he wants to see me so helplessly that he takes it out in boasting about me to those damn natives that can make him hang his head—over his loose daughter—or his daughter loose among dirty foreigners—
as you like. See a little? It's crazy and the minute I'm there, it won't have mattered except to me, but what ho, *la puissance* [the power] of symbolism. So I say to my greedy self that we'll be coming south and lingering and it'll be all the more fun for former abstemiosity.

She will deny herself for father and family, a literary puritan à la Isabel Archer. But care as she does what her people think, all she can promise the man she wants to marry is to see his play at Harvard: "So this way I'll be home in May—it's all there is—there is lots more—and although met and beset by Father, Mother, and Brother I'll go to Cambridge to see that persistent play and its papa. Don't throw me out. I've seen so many family formations and I live one across geography and if you pull my right ear I say Mamma and if you pull my left I say DaDa and when you pinch my nose I yell Bub-ba!" Stress is eased when her thesis is abruptly accepted:

> The last damn professor—Pole—kept it three weeks and then—oh these inevitable *recoltèd* [circulated] felicitations are the worst of all—the *recteur* has sealed it—the doyen has deposed it—the eight cumulative inscriptions are paid for and the atrocity goes to press Monday or Tuesday. I have to publish—and it will cost at least 5,000 francs (odious). Then the *soutenance* [defense]. I'm afraid I won't get away before the first of May. There's other details. But O Dos I am so glad to be *à peu près* [almost] quits. I got into such a mess that I wonder if I'll ever entirely recover.

She had spoken of doing a second Ph.D., in history, with a dissertation on Anatole France's influence, but Crystal made no such effort, would not again believe in her academic future. In the moment she exfloriates with Easter detail: "The sun" shines through "the music in the cathedral" on "little chocolate lambs in baskets"; she is *"lilting* and cascading with things to tell you," but "Here we are in the stuffy salon playing chess," she writes, "Constantin and a fellow Rumanian exchanging Rumanian profanities."

Dos has had a very tempting invitation:

> Look Crys, let me know all plans. We must see each other this
> spring. Gerald Murphy has asked me to go sailing with him in the

Mediterranean in June, to Greece, Cyprus, etc. I just can't pass it up. He and I and two Russians. I'd learn Russian and seamanship at one fell swoop.

You're not the only one who's had headaches. I've spent a large part of winter dying *d'inanition* [of starvation] as Casanova says—that is except for my accursed inner-outer novel-composing delirium that has taken most of my energy. But slighted Aphrodite [mentioned to her before] has been punishing me with various glooms and neurasthenias. It all blew up in a vast explosion and I went for a walk on Cape Cod & returned feeling vastly better to a last attack [on the novel].

I salute you doctor Portia *expartibus, e pluribus, ext se vinculis sub muros* etc. [all nonsense]. Don't shoot till you see the whites of their eyes.

Dos

She replies with "Whoops Dos and *quinze* [fifteen of them] for *le* Gerald Murphy. . . . I was so glad that I fell off the stove (where I sit to read letters while the maid brushes about) and tore a stocking, my last *entiére* [whole one]—and then I was awfully encouraged because being pretty damn sure that I'm hopelessly in love with you or at least hankering for the sight and to be seen by you, I can cascade with pleasure over a prospect that leaves me out. It's a good sign, isn't it?" She is being a good sport, and may feel less guilty about going home when he has something fun to do. She sets down a few "clear clauses" about her schedule:

My infernal printer having guaranteed the job for 8 days is taking exactly 28, so God knows when I'll get out. But I shall wait a word from you telling me to hurry—or to loiter—depending on which side of the *Atlantique* we achieve our slender little spring session. I think April 27th for the *soutenance*—leave here May first or second. Paris a few days (I want a month). That accursed *SUFFREN* sails the

13th, the *DE GRASSE* on the 6th (too breathless!) and *ILE DE FRANCE* the 20th—the *DE GRASSE* again May 30th. My family is wild and they are right. I ought to burn to be there too—but gosh, I can trickle down thru and home it [by ship from Naples to Texas] if you're out of N.Y.

Figurez-vous [imagine] that a pal, a Texas boy, invited me on just the sailing tour that your Murphy purposes, and in June. If I had dreamed of you in the same waters I couldn't have resisted it—and if I thought you'd have the desire, *le quoi* [the wherewithal], etc. to feed and clothe and comfort me next winter I'd hail him yet. Figurez-vous—and Greece too! (I think he has typhoid by now.)

She then makes an offer she won't repeat: "But if you'll take the responsibility and the challenge I'll wait for you in an Italian depot—or *pension*. I could never go home afterwards, not because of the scandal but the heartlessness." Dos wasn't wholly comfortable leaving her for what turned into his Riviera summer with Picasso and the Murphys, nor was he prepared (as she undoubtedly knew) for the definitive step of an Italian rendezvous. What would she have done if he'd taken her up on this? She had overpaid the debt of love to her father. With an ironic sense of propriety, Crystal writes: "*Alors* [It follows that], if you're not leaving New York before the 1st of June, I think my cue is to rush over, wish you bon voyage, and hie me to the familial banquet *pour ma prodigalité* (biblical, dear, not financial though both). So cable me here, the first, second, or third even, and afterwards 4 *rue Chevreuse* Paris, to hurry or to linger, and I'll do whatever hits me hardest." She urges him to enjoy himself as she prepares to return home:

It's just fine Dos, this Mediterranean sailing. You'll sun all this narsty *hiver* [winter] out of your system forever. I'd've given anything that was *mine* to have gone off to New York in time for Spring. As 'tis, have an idea for the narrow margin that I will manage, and write it [their dates together] to me in Paris. Brudge [her brother] will

do the meeting and all that. His name is A. A. Ross and his address
Jersey City Hospital—that is a N.Y. *post restante*. What's your phone
number? When a whole life is not enough, we're just nuts to put all its
meaning into [one moment]. Heigh ho for the salutation of the dawn,
with just a photograph to tell our troubles tooooo [a line
from a popular song quoted in *Manhattan Transfer*].

"I'm not going to have any more troubles," she says, throwing off
a pun on *Ça ne vaut pas la peine* [it's not worth the trouble]. But her
defense is one more time delayed:

Oh damn it all Dos this is to say that the *soutenance* is put off
again. *Un professeur* who has to take time to read the thesis—[and]
didn't—finds he has *une affaire* [some business] *à Paris le Samedi* [on
Saturday]. So I'm sailing on the *de Grasse* on the thirtieth. I am tired
now and so damned stifled *chez Madame* and *ailleurs* [in Madame's
home and everywhere else]. These particular limitations and
rigidities are getting me wild—loony—and Friday is the first of May. I
can't get out before the 10th now or later even.

How's the novel? I'll send you a copy of the thing I've perpetrated
but for God's sake don't read anything except the life and the *cadres*
[categories of O. Henry's work] and the themes. That will cure you
and wither me.

I don't know which way to turn Dos and I can't keep still and I
can't fall off and I can't wake up—and I ain't no comfort to ye. Crys

Bestirring himself, Dos tried to ride to the rescue. He handed in
Manhattan Transfer to his editor at Harper, Eugene Saxton, and in what
has to have been a phone call—Crystal saved important cables—proposed
to meet in Paris to celebrate her degree. They'd have two and a half
weeks. "Whoops Dos—this is fine," she writes:

on a quand même un peu de chance! [one has all the same a little luck!]
Ho then, the fifteenth or the thirteenth. Take a fast boat—there are

Crys Makes a Decision—Dos to the Rescue

reasons! I'll be twiddlin' my thumbs round 4 *rue de Chevreuse.* That's a safe address anyway. I'll be there on Monday the 12th.

It's cold as blue crickets and the wind hoots outside the colored glass windows of the municipal bath, but Madame is making herself a purple silk *combinaison* [slip] and we have twisty sprays of May flowers all about the Rose room. I've been reading for the *soutenance,* since they added another member to the jury—a French lit guy from Paris—and I will be so unutterably glad to be over it before you come. Onward Christian Soldiers!

Bon Voyage. You're a whiz to make it, *soi le bienvenu!* [be welcome]. You can send things for me to do as I go by—if there's proof to correct or such. I'm *en tran* [in motion], just get yourself onto the ocean. I invite you to lunch on the Eiffel Tower.

"When you get this I'll be in Paris. The wild hawk to the windswept sky," she scrawls on the formal announcement of her successful defense and the awarding of her degree, the hawk's flight marked by an ascending cleft. Her belief that they can spend their lives together seems justified.

Interlude in Paris—Strasbourg Loyalties—Arrival Stateside

DOS PASSOS WASN'T COMING to 4 rue de Chevreuse. He was sick, and as she left New York for Texas a month later, he would succumb to rheumatic fever, the onset of which can be four or five weeks preceded by a strep throat and temperature. It was his first severe bout of the disease since the fall of 1919. Finishing *Manhattan Transfer* under all the pressure wore him out. "When luck is against you everything goes wrong," he'd worried. For seventeen days in the spring of 1925 Crys camped out on the Left Bank, in Dos's absence fostered by the Hemingways. Hadley said she "had developed" during the year, joking that Dos's taste in women was better than Benchley's, his girl being Dorothy Parker.

Crystal read the proofs of the Boni and Liveright *In Our Time* for Hemingway, making "suggestions—grammar not style—accepted," except when, she amusedly recalled, she inserted commas he forthwith removed. Thinking these short stories "incomparable," she was glad when he ditched the lowercase title on which McAlmon insisted for the Three Mountains Press volume. She read "Big Two-Hearted River" in the first issue of *This Quarter,* which came out when she was in Paris in May '25, and agreed with Hemingway it was his best to date. He had Americanized *The Waste Land* as the burned-over country with black grasshoppers and the verdant river bottom where the narrator presides as fisher-king. Crystal matched this text to her sense of the man, someone "intensely curious" but "little occupied with general ideas, not given to the impersonal." She admired the clarity and simplicity with which he defined "courage (physical); fear (moral)." What he said to her about art, in a not quite impassive manner, was that "ugly is bracing not dispiriting" and "most pain bound up with joy," lessons she had been learning. When they spoke of her student world in Alsace he was "very aware of stresses—injustices—the awkward position of [her] friends who were socialists but adored and emulated Americans." All this is behind Jake's aside to Cohn about the swell girl they can visit in Strasbourg.

Hemingway's changes over the years as "fame became of him" didn't prepare Crys and Dos for the put-downs of writers in *A Moveable Feast*. Crystal admired *No More Parades* (1925), the second volume of the trilogy *Parade's End,* and when Ford Maddox Ford had her to lunch with Hadley, rather liked his manner of a British officer turned aesthete. She couldn't have imagined that Hem, having struggled with Ford's magazine over the *Making of Americans,* at the end of his life would describe the editor as a fraud and windbag. She began to lose faith in him when he chose Pauline Pfeiffer over Hadley in 1926. Dos, though Pauline's admirer, proposed to knock Hemingway and Hadley's heads together unless Hem at once declared himself a Mormon. Crystal had no idea that he was uneasy with Stein's sexuality while happily absorbing her literary influence. Walking with Crys to tea at 27 rue de Fleurus, he praised her brains as he did in a well-known letter to Wilson of the same year. When Stein asked what the young woman thought of bullfighting, Crystal tactfully called it an art that was "soundest" in its dignity, in being "groomed." Invited to stand in for her hostess at what she would recall as Bumby's French christening, Crystal took back to Texas a baptismal certificate dated March 16, 1924, which was six months before she had met the Hemingways in

Paris. The confusion plain in these dates is no longer subject to clarification. The certificate, signed by Killian A. Stimpson, the Episcopal priest who presided over the ceremony at St. Luke's-in-the-Garden, lists three sponsors, Capt. E. E. Dorman Smith, Miss Gertrude Stein, and Miss Alice Toklas. Why would my mother have been given one of the copies of this document, presumably one that was set aside for Stein? Stein might have missed the occasion, either reluctantly—or was she perhaps disqualified as a Jew?

In notes after Hemingway's suicide in 1962, Crystal recalls the Fitzgeralds' visit in May '25. Hadley had been nervous about inviting the fashionable pair for a meal over the sawmill. "I don't want my baby to have a nagging mother," she said to Crys, "but O this wallpaper and those Fitzgeralds coming for lunch." When they met, Zelda "embarrassed" Hadley by confiding "that the man [the French aviator Edouard Jozan] had killed himself for her." (He did not. He died of natural causes in 1981.) Hadley had promised "to stay put and stay rested" while Hem was "off to Lyon with Scott," but the first night she and Crystal, Zelda and Hem's friend Bill Smith—whose older sister Kate would marry Dos in 1929—went out to Montmartre. Crystal recalled that "the Negro entertainer (female) accused me of being from the South—why?" She flattened vowels like the "a" in "water," yet otherwise lacked a southern accent. Crystal had hated racial segregation since she was twelve, when her formidable Aunt Stella, her father's older sister, slapped her face for speaking to a Negro in a Chicago hotel. After the party with Zelda and Bill Smith broke up, she notes, "I danced alone at [illegible]." A day later came "Hem's report on tour with Scott Fitzgerald. His hypochondria. Taking temperature with wall thermometer [in *A Moveable Feast* it's a bath thermometer]. Their bad nights drinking—Hem driving." Crystal had heard Fitzgerald speak to a Columbia class about *The Beautiful and Damned* in 1922 but didn't know he'd brought Hemingway a copy of *Gatsby*, published in April '25. Back in the States she found the novel dazzling.

She never formally connected Hemingway's early stories with her dissertation's claim that Americans—a young, impatient, and curious race with a fast-paced life—were perfecting the genre, but it supports her judgments of *In Our Time* and *Men without Women* in the *Dallas News*. At the beginning of *Le conteur américain O. Henry et l'art de Maupassant* Crystal stresses the art of the miniature, quoting the seventeenth-century critic Boileau that a faultless sonnet is the aesthetic equal of a long poem. The sonnet's concision—like that of the short story—*"ne tolère ni désordre dans la composition, ni relachment dans le style."* ("There is no continuum between the mediocre and the worst," Boileau put it.) This dictum hadn't helped her with O. Henry, whose anecdotes failed to amuse, while Maupassant, the "master technician," left Crystal cold. She put the dissertation behind her, stacking copies in the trunk for Lockhart. But the French critic's authority confirmed her preference of Hemingway's early stories to *The Sun Also Rises*. An Aristotelian concept of action as the source of character rather than the other way around may have led Crystal to that early judgment.

On the *De Grasse* she looked back to Madame Epp's Strasbourg household. Marie had been "frightened and ignorant" when first pregnant, she'd told Crys, had "carried coal hoppers—bounced over the clothes basket in attic" to bring on a miscarriage; "her sister helped hide the fetus." Pregnant again in '24–'25, this time "the father ran her off," but she proudly said, "I'll have my baby and I'll wheel him in a carriage." ("Baby had been born on the train to Lyon," Crystal notes.) Madame Epp, who married at seventeen and lost her husband in her twenties, said she didn't have affairs so as not to create families of half brothers and half sisters. Yet she had been a mother to her American guest, had spoken of Mimma's beauty in a wedding photograph. Crystal honored maternity and wanted to be good at it.

Madame Epp had been unable to mother Constantin, and their relations deteriorated near the end of Crystal's stay. "When he was ill (sinus) he had a caller [who] was perfumed, rouged. Madame's outrage—opened windows—told C. the man could never come again." Constantin later wrote to Crystal "that he had a woman in, so's to get thrown out." His mother "set him up to a room *en ville* [in town], beside

Mme. Epp's bower and chapel." Yet the rebellious princeling—who called his father the prince "bourgeois" but proposed to market the name for a Citroen—turned out to be no lightweight. He would distinguish himself as an air ace during World War II, surviving to lead an American air-rescue team behind the German lines. Constantin told Crystal her children would be fortunate, and when he took her to her train for Paris, in the aisle handed her a locket-sized framed engraving of an old woman, signed Rembrandt, under it the handwritten title, "Rembrandt's Mother," saying, "You ought to have this." She would one day give it to her elder son, telling me that Hemingway admired the miniature, as Dos did when he saw it in New York.

Dos Passos, her father, and her brother met her on the pier at Hoboken. Bubba, then doing his residency in the Jersey City hospital, had cruelly teased her in adolescence, but she failed to foresee he'd tell their father what was up, and that Doctor would be waiting on the dock. There are no details about this moment. Dos's joints were painfully swollen from the maladies that pursued him, and Crys insisted on staying in New York. Respectably taking a room at the Lafayette in Manhattan, she looked after him for the better part of a week, and they went to the theater when he was up to it. They were again separated when her father, back in Lockhart, trumped Dos's illness by phoning that her mother's heart condition was worse and Mimma gravely ill. As Crystal hurried to Texas, Dos was overtaken by rheumatic fever, he writes in a penciled note to Lockhart:

> Dear Crys: Thanks ever so much for the fruit. It was very sweet of
> you to send it. I found myself with a nasty inflammatory rheumatism
> and have been in bed ever since I last saw you. Damned annoying.
> However I seem to be improving and have faint hopes of getting off
> on the Homer Friday night.
>
> Horrible was it not to get this outrageous disease? How are you?
> Do let me hear about everything. French address will be Norton-
> Harjes Paris.
> Love Dos

She didn't let him hear "about everything," nor did she know he'd fallen seriously ill, not getting off till two weeks later. Unable to catch the *Homer* on June 30, he reported on his malady in a registered letter dated that day, containing "$10 I owe you": "Dear Crys: I'm just beginning to creep about with inflammatory rheumatism—a most hellish complaint ever since that Sunday you left for Texas. This certainly is not my lucky spring. Wrote you weeks ago but I never got it mailed. I'll mail it when I find it. I feel like having myself dumped in an ashcan." The emotional and physical had merged, for in both notes, sent two weeks apart, he succumbs as she leaves him. Dos and Hart Crane, his neighbor at Columbia Heights, sometimes dined together, and they looked out for each other. "When Crane was seriously drunk," records a chronicler of literary Brooklyn, "Dos Passos would try to talk him into turning in for the night." The poet "would pretend to be persuaded and then sneak out to cruise the bars, sometimes returning with a bruised face." Crane wrote to the *Seven Arts* critic Waldo Frank that Dos Passos's two bouts of fever "almost finished him." Hoping to "get off on July 3rd," again Dos asked Crystal to write "care Norton-Harjes, 14 *Place Vendôme*." He wanted to know, "How are Texas and the Middle Buster?"

PART III

Madame Butterfly

DOS KNEW HE HAD lost to Doctor Ross when Crys went back to Texas, but she never let him know how lost she was after getting there. There was no familial banquet for the prodigal daughter. "Doctor tricked me" was all she ever said about going home, for her mother's condition seemed unchanged. Not due to teach until the second summer session, she could have taken care of Dos a little longer. She'd once humorously asked him not "to let me do a poor Butterfly." Now the melodrama was reality.

The first of three letters to him that Texas summer is written on the stationery of Austin's fashionable new hotel:

Dear Dos, the cross shows where I am now. The unctuous manager may hoist me higher [to a higher floor] tonight. I've been to the library and hauled home great hunks of booking to eat. I am giving two courses, one at 7:00 am, Short Story Mutations, one at 8:00 am, French Realistic Novel.

People came in the office this morning to ask about them. I left. O my French flame-and-white-sportsuit flauntiness is caving in, curlin' up. And the ridiculous isolation of my grand manner hoteling. Thinking about you and your way helps.

I must learn a lot that is read and spare words. Signs like that *Spahr Brot* [Dutch for "spare bread," a sign they'd seen in Holland] should be put up all over universities. I am on the Social Committee and trying to resign was worse than serving can be. *Spahr Verben!* No dancing. Too bad, they close down the gym [in the summer]. I had fun in my room—did a Felix the movie cat you know?—to *Thais* syncopated (*La Meditation Meme* [itself]). That sort of thing just dazes Alsatians, till you want to jump flat foot *au milieu des fauteuil d'orchestre* [into the center of the orchestra seats] and say "boo" adequately!

I have to scratch up a Say [lecture] on Balzac. Listen, I've an idea. I'll bet it was never practiced in a *collich* course. Don't hash literary history. Don't resume. Selflessness: let 'um do it. Say only cues. I wonder if I can. I've nothing to lose (that's Texas and CRR) and my soul to save.

Dos, I trust you know enough to care for your black symptoms. That rheuming has awful *suites* [aftereffects]. Have fun for me and music and swimmin' and pictures painted and if you've the notion or the time come home this way—Galveston. I'll meet you, and don't be afraid of me—I'll probably marry the Attorney General. Crys

Her teaching duties behind her, at summer's end she writes on a train "riding west out of Ft. Worth": "Sweet Dos, I am not a strange creature, and share your hellish summers in their simmering please. We must not lose our exchanging just because of my arrested development— I've corrected that—and your precipitations." We aren't privy to Dos's "precipitations" and may wonder just how Crystal "corrected" her development. "I like to think you're out now, over it, and on," she tells him. "Take me with you as you go, and I'll do likewise." She would live long enough to use this as a farewell line with people she loved, but it was an awkward letter at an awkward time, and she began all over again: "Sweet Dos, I am not up to anything. I have hardly been home since July 1st, a week in seven snatches perhaps. I keep moving territorially

Madame Butterfly

and I seem every few weeks to crash thru, to get new leases. Guess I am a process or a kinetic theory or do I mean centrifugal force, and you?" She returns to the drive between Lockhart and Austin:

> I left Lockhart, and rode up the Middle Buster across a sunset. Dry fields, bare as before Spring, gorgeous jellied clouds. I remember. Willows along Onion Creek and cedars even. Then the hills. I was wondering—dreadful—then Dos it was a lilt, a triumph, a gorgeous preposterous antidote. I lived at the Steven F. Austin downtown, the only gilt-edged sky-high fine hotel. New outdoor dining a surprise. I dwelt there the whole time amid legislative lobbying, riding cool and high. Complications be damned and were. Hotel like an ocean liner rising aloof of one or two storied Congress evenings. Longhorn Roof ablaze with jazz. Capitol Dome oh lovely white stone glow. A light from outside—soft searchers. My long closed genteelly shabby car. A visiting girl whom we affianced—and not me—to the rising young attorney general. I'm half sorry—you would have liked visiting us in the Governor's Mansion! A comic opera. But then the years after to be worthy or unworthy or divorced in which order.

The visiting girl was Mildred Paxton, boon companion during Crystal's year at Columbia, when Mildred was in journalism school. She married Dan Moody, the attorney general, and when Dan successfully campaigned for governor of Texas was "inducted, not unwillingly, to the limelight," Crystal dubbing herself "permanent lady-in-waiting." Crystal tells Dos how she and Mildred had "hopped a freight at 116th St. and Riverside and couldn't get off until Yonkers." Decades afterward, during my graduate years at Columbia, when the ladies bragged of this exploit I trembled for them, for the only way to catch a freight at 116th Street then was by a two-foot jump down onto the train before it went beneath the overpass a few feet away. Apparently in 1926, my mother had scared friends by diving off a railroad bridge over the Brazos River, encountering no plowshare at the bottom.

Madame Butterfly

Imagining life without Dos's love, in France she'd wondered "what makes undercurrents keep coming?," answering, "If they took themselves off to the sea, the top would fall in." "Wasn't that a fine walk we had to Delft?" she asks Dos, her sense of self alternately unraveling and recovering:

> Dos, I have crashed thru at least 4 times since New York. Each one I
> think "The Core" and bejabbers it isn't so rotten after all. Aren't you
> glad, that I know it, I mean? And you Ichabod—and you? But what
> do we care what we are? I am sorry not to have clarified for and with
> you I think twas by you.
> Crys

She has found (shades of Constantin Cantacuzino!) a new young companion, a Mississippian with a taste for books and the florid full name Lucius Quintus Cincinnatus Mirabeau Lamar. Her end-of-summer letter tells Dos: "I had a wreck with a Negro overland—hubs and fenders. Big crowd—'Lynch the damn nigger.' I suggested sweetly that they better hang me up too, the collision having been entirely mine, and the remark cost my Dad insurance damages!"

In this summer's third letter, also begun on a train, she is adrift in a land that lives on oil gushers and Prohibition liquor, before air-conditioning. She piles up the details:

> This, Dos, is Abilene. [The trip] involves small nieces and nephews to
> the circus, fathers to football games, mothers calling, sisters-in-law
> bridging, and eligible young men to Buffalo Gap for fried chicken and
> what is called "Reisling wine." Mildred and I like each other; so we
> ride it. Men are coming from Dallas tomorrow and we shall do Cedar
> Gap, if this rain abates and it's a norther. Otherwise I've a red dress
> for sitting before the fire. Because I like Mildred this is a rambling
> where others have been dashing about. I spent my fewish earnings
> for books and I've crated some ranchward. So if I have an objective

it is there to read—to see if I can rest. I haven't ever wanted to more. Now the need isn't based on fatigue whatsoever, but this chronic confusion.

Oh shucks, we could coin sentences but they won't incorporate into paragraphs; so here's the jumble: Hot days, whiskey hangovers, sounding blue brass skies, white jagged tin clouds, cool nights, robin's egg skies, hard-boiled. Dry. Riding across looming dry fields to corn-whiskey floated dances and back before dawn when cottontail rabbits jump and gravel crunches under balloon tires and those who haven't passed out sing "All alone, I'm so alone" in whiskeyed tenors.

Texans of this era liked to boast they could hold their liquor, and Crystal was young enough to be sure she could outdrink the boys:

Usually I was sole survivor, my capacity or my will being above the local average. So I drove and knew night in the oil fields, derricks sometimes alight. At Ganders Slough, Dale, Lytton Springs, Prairie Lea—you enjoy the names? You'd not have endured the parties, but I throve.

Hotel Roof Gardens. "Our gang" takes a "suite" down one floor. Cahoots with house detectives and black bellhops—contrived or contriven. Bathtubs of beer, clothes closets of prescription stuff and corn and orange tequila at a stretch. I learned amazed. Collegiate jazz to float and cover. Everybody risking his liberty, his stomach, and his peace of family. Mine quietly assures herself that I might commit vague rowdiness but would not, could not touch the cup. Where were we? Oh yes. One of those commotions per 24 hours with a bounding life thrown in did give me little internal staccatos that suggested abstinence from nothing. Favorite bootleggers. Horrid stuff and timid way of having it.

Stuffy parlors, lamplit in farmhouses. Hot iron clods, their cracks leering at clouds that threatened rain and hadn't let any fall in more than a year. Not a swiggin' bit of cotton. No fruit. Few watermelons.

Madame Butterfly

A joyless Negro day. Mexican renters sneaking away, entire families at night, away from debts toward work—in the Panhandle—and they've only begun, the consequences of the drought.

Fun to see how the oil lubricates and does not. "Field pretty well defined now, north and south of town." Steadily pumping shallow wells. High grade oil. The townspeople are no richer, except spottedly here and there the riskers. But the town is a channel. Things go thru and even on it. There are even a few people one does not know. Although one soon knows all about them.

The hectic hooch parties were cramped once for a temporary die downing. The blond young daughter, older than you'd think, of a boarding-house lady down the street [from her home in Lockhart] had been going with a married man. Happy go-lucky kid married to a violently Episcopalian woman who seemed to be always visiting even at home. The father shot the happy one dead between the fourth and fifth ribs. I liked him, poor devil. Most people did. Yet all the town felicits the stupid old father for protecting the honor of his home; any Southern gentleman should do as much. Father might be embarrassed to know baby girl's going at least half the way.

Sharing this with Dos, Crystal surely knew he would never come to Texas to get her, even with Hemingway riding shotgun.

Oh about Lockhart, that was and is, like so many places doubtless, hot—oh roasting! Not even water for basting. I realize how that culinary process with its gravy helps, as we sauce sweltering diagonally across seven demi-torrents to utter drought. We were building a Masonic Temple. Without a dance roof. Expensive rain-proof tinning instead. Then pray for rain. Many important men came for the funny cornerstone service. Dad's guests opened the *grand* East! Whatever. Seven or so of them stayed several days with us. Meaning 21 meals a day, plus ice water between. I liked having them. All of us did, except perhaps Ava the cook—our hub— a Negro without humor. She went vacationing in a Ford with 5 clean pairs of stockings. I functioned. Now she says to others, "Don't tell Miss Cryssie but I can't find nothing." Well my element is more sweeping and I mops best—but Madame's regimen has told on me and I swear I am domestic and do many little things around the house—sometimes.

Crystal would tirelessly sing "Doctor's" praises to her children and grandchildren, but in this letter to Dos Passos he is a domestic tyrant, she reduced to a rebellious adolescent, hard-won Ph.D. in hand:

> My sweet, sweet father I do like. He disapproves, his eyebrows
> pulverize luckless callers, but the only dissension where I have
> not just taken my way or made him think me generous not to,
> was over sleeping in the hammock in the back yard. I meant to all
> unsuspecting one evening, and was told in conclusion, that so long
> as I comport I am given "the protection of the home." But I am
> denied the shelter of the barn. "Sleep in a hammock—20 paces from
> the back steps—Crystal are you crazy?" I have enjoyed it. Ridden it
> because I have hardly cared. Jumping jackrabbits don't let me begin
> to. Lockhart is deeeelightful never the accent on either of the other
> syllables. Maybe—and how should I know? I've been demi-dutiful in
> deed, utterly un otherwise.

The conflict between her father's values and those she had come into with Dos seemed "between my instincts and my origins," as she put it to me, and she hoped to reconcile them in marriage. To Dos she writes, "I am not going to teach—refused up and down the scale":

> People think that mad, for why is one educated at whatever? The
> better to teach, my dear. I said Poppycock of Ph.D.'s one day in my
> office. The society Editoress capitalized it under Youth, Beauty and
> Culture—yes dear—and a thinly unctuous President invited me to
> luncheon. We talked of trout fishing and commencement accidents
> and I wore yellow stockings. Duck-like.

Madame Butterfly

Swimming I contrived but not very liltily. Distance and dust. Mud in Austin! I swam in cold stained-glass water every morning at 5:30 toward that seven o'clock class, often at broad boiling noon, sometimes by moonlight [all this at Barton Springs, a much-loved reservoir fed by the Colorado River in Austin].

Lucius and I went to a little German town northwest of Austin where you must go when/if you come. The Plano River goes by. A train comes in but none goes out. Then we gypsied lately thru the westish and Tuscany hills. Marble Falls. Cypress Mills. Spicewood. Liberty Hill [her younger brother Raleigh would own the RRR Ranch at Liberty Hill, where, at ninety-two, Crystal began an exercise regimen after hip replacement]. This is fine country. So high and circular and flat, its openness and yet definite horizon reflected in the people. Nice people. Sweet. But brittley Puritan. Sabbath is Sabbath.

My soul, what's the point to fence in this big country? The little slim posts go pointing about. I've been quilting this craziness several days. Gorgeous October days. I am busy playing my role for a most appreciative and generous audience. Set out violets this morning with Mildred's mother in their cemetery lot and golfed this afternoon with her Dad. Poker tonight. But we mountain-climbed Sunday. I wish you could see Mildred in her golf togs swinging thru Texas. She is brown-eyed and amber haired.

I've been reading such a hodgepodge about things I haven't seen that my mind is Russian salad. We're driving to Dallas tomorrow—200 miles—for the next day's football game and festivities. I have had enough and am restless to be alone and on. You'd better send this letter back to me. See how I am brave. I do not want nor care of the stamping. And you have always capable envelopes. I'll maybe send you postals from thru the looking-glass places. You may keep the postals!!

She is talking around their relationship's end: "Dos I'm sorry about your infernal rheumatism. I hope you hunted down the source, convalesced

Madame Butterfly

afloat, and are—if you like—Morocco bound, among stimulating people and other stimulants. You said to me you were a solitaire—but I liked our double game and I owe you because I see I cheated but that is why I won. I wish you a winning." She admits to have lost when, with failure all around, she adds: "Sometimes I miss you Dos—although I seem always to have you—although I never did. My very love to the Hemingways. Bless Hadley. Crys."

Dos's rheumatism flared up in Morocco, where he investigated a tribal rebellion against the French (it fizzled when the Riff leader was captured and sent off in Napoleon's footsteps to Reunion Island). He digested reviews of *Manhattan Transfer*. In response to Crystal's impressionistic missive, he writes: "Just got a wonderfully strange letter from you. Kid you can write—but I make you out less and less. Maybe we'll have to go to Mexico to find out, but the finding out would all be on my side—honest you've got me guessing." Saying "I don't have the slightest stock in the 'rotten-at-the-core' claim," he reports he is "in excellent health drinking a cognac *a l'eau* [with water] *Chez François* [a café] waiting for my girlfriend [herself] and everything is as logical as a madhouse." He expects her to be there without asking her to come. There is little about his life—"Just came up from a couple of weeks of sailing. That's a damn sight more worthwhile than sitting chattering in cafes." He likes thinking of her as a "wordfellow": "It's amazing what a vivid picture your letter gave me. I feel as if I'd spent a week with you in Texas. Take a drink of white mule or whatever you call it at the next nocturnal party. Why the hell should I send the letter back? I will if you want." In the end the mask of detachment drops. "There are little stoves [in] the cafes and Paris is very cozy in the fog but I wish I was in Ballywack [a Victorian euphemism for Hell, likely used by Dos's mother, as it was by my grandmother]," he writes. Back in New York he found himself celebrated for the novel but had to get along without a five- or ten-dollar bill to his name, he told a friend. He worked in a theater group, returned to radical politics.

Crystal survived her encounters with the New York train and Texas railroad bridge, and stretched the patriarchal bond when she successfully escaped from her corner via teaching. "Swaddled as I am in provincialism, swatched 'in protection,' tethered to tradition," she wrote to Dos some months afterward, "I've compromised again, but not gracefully, being coerced":

I'm going to teach, to profess comparative literature in Dallas, not Austin. Yan Yan I swore I wouldn't—and spent all my own money for books from a boy I'm trying to help [make his way] in Houston—Lamar. Patron of the Arts aha! That's me. And drug around a stove-inside. Still I thought I could manage—but I can't.

So suddenly the job offered, at S.M.U. I'm keeping something [illegible] from you. It's a Methodist school. Mencken will be scouting me for some of his formulae. And I won't stay home and coddle my complexion and my filial sentiments, and I won't visit another visit—and so. Dallas is a big rather throbbing town, with the world's most inevitable Main Street. My social affiliations are of the best, if it's husbandry that insinuates or lures or leers or is logical.

Having agreed "to teach 3 courses of my own choosing in the field of General Literature," she adds, "I ought to learn a phrase or two." Howard Mumford Jones, her mentor at the University of Texas, was known as "G-Lit Jones" and doubtless helped with the job. Jones would be called to Harvard in 1936, and it may have been through him that Crystal was later approached about teaching at Mount Holyoke, where her son Ross Dabney (a Harvard Ph.D.) would have a position during the 1960s. Yet as she leaves for Dallas her situation is "strangely bitter":

I have nothing to say to more than 3 people on earth, and I'm to stand and talk to mobs 2 hours a day against time and culture. Men scratch to live don't they? Oh well it's worth it. I swear Dos that I cannot get my fingers 'round the fare to New York, but I am buying a rather volatile car, and am going to pay for it in the course of the nine months, that is for a controlling interest, and have that means of motion. And I plan to learn to fly a plane. I think that's important and haven't been able to achieve it. Fly with me someday? I'll be the eyes if you'll be the map.

Did she—like Wilson—link Dos's myopia to the practice of documenting his characters' inner lives through externals? She had envisioned their marriage as a partnership in which she contributed to his art. Her health too had taken a beating:

> I'm on the upslope of sundry surgeries. Still prone but far from prostrate and beginning to peer out. Once permitted to stir, I plan to launch straightway into the air. I learned that experience is the best teacher as to tonsils, that more phoatrophine in the arm is an amazing cheap intoxication, that to have one's side anesthetized, to feel one's side pass out and watch its adjustment and count the stitches in and on catgut, that's a new rhythm! I took locals, not caring to babble before the home talent in surgery. Brudge is transcendently skillful. He's home from Jersey City to stay south. I'm glad to convalesce, but post-operative invoices are tedious. The horror—no swimming and little dancing before Thanksgiving. My students will probably absorb my energies anyway. I'm *Dr.* Ross— O Strasboroooo!

Her "family-in-being" are "a riot. 'Among the Rosses with Gun and Camera.' I have a new enthusiasm, Mother—never liked her before." Elsewhere she reports that three days with Mimma helped her to define domesticity: "It's a finger exercise, and maddens them as is and isn't musical. A kind of rhythm, even a tune. Mother's a melody." Crystal remained skeptical of women's concentration and focus: "I should like to be preoccupied, Dos, instead of forever carrying in my head the things of interest while I add another column. But we give ourselves these little fires, we scattering females, to keep us warm. I wonder if we burn away dross, or conscience fiber, or just add layers of ashes." Crystal's next words would help Dos Passos dramatize the figure of Daughter: "I continue to crash thru, but as a serial picture crashing to the core. Serial prolonged for emotional vortices—of course it's just that. I have no adequate channel for varied energies, and no point of view nor a sensor! By the time we're 100 we'll know how, won't we?" This is the unspoken refrain of much of their correspondence of these years. "Meanwhile take the day off in my, shall we say, honor. Snatch it from eternity if that means a tailspin above Mt. Sinai." Having seen herself buffeted about without a core, in the Protestant romantic tradition, she grandly conjures up death in a "tailspin above Mt. Sinai." Dos appropriates the imagery when Daughter, abandoned and desperate in her pregnancy, persuades the drunken French aviator to do loop-a-loops above Paris.

Two Marriages

CRYSTAL HAD A SUCCESSFUL teaching year at Southern Methodist University (SMU), keeping "intense possession" of her apartment and enjoying the car she was paying for. In Dallas in the fall of '26 she encountered a young lawyer whose dry wit she liked. The story is that they met under a rug at a party, crawling from different directions to introduce themselves. They are said to have emerged with aplomb. Lewis M. Dabney Jr. was a classically educated rebel of the hard-drinking postwar set—"Here's to October, drink him down," he wrote enthusiastically soon after. He was born in Dallas in 1899 of a Virginia family. His father was a lawyer, his grandfather the Calvinist theologian who was chief of staff to Stonewall Jackson in the Civil War. Dr. Dabney later went south to help found the University of Texas. Lewis, preparing for college at Lawrenceville while his sister was at nearby Bryn Mawr, graduated from Princeton in 1921, Harvard Law three years later. In the Princeton of the "gentleman's C" he picked up a song about liquor, "the servant of man" ("Down in the city of booze / You live and do just as you choose"). In passing he identified his favorite department as the Fire Department. He was involved with the *Tiger*, the humor magazine Fitzgerald had helped edit several years before. Dean Roscoe Pound's famous introduction to Harvard Law was a memorable moment in Lewis's youth, reassuring him "it was alright to be smart." He made the *Law Review,* and there was a story in the *Dallas News.*

He had expected to go home and practice law with his father, but the senior Lewis Dabney died after a sudden stroke early in the summer of 1923, perhaps a preface to that Lewis suffered in the fall of 1992. Telling himself that he might have liked to be a chemist, the son stoically returned to a position in his father's firm. Dallas lawyering was vivified by assignments in the booming East Texas oil fields. He wrote to future Supreme Court justice Felix Frankfurter, who had become a mentor at Harvard, about the land law created by "some of our early judges, who were really great men," imaginative "old fellows to whose work I help myself." This letter mentions "the gambler's kick of dealing with big money (even though it is not my own), and the further pleasure of having to do with only two kinds of people, a very high class and cheerful pirates."

The Dallas he returned to from the North, however, wasn't the same without the man he told Crystal was "three-quarters of myself nine times magnified." His mother was loftily conventional. The hole in his life left room for Crystal's large personality, and he fell passionately in love, proposing at the end of "a gorgeous fall." In a letter to Dos she calls Lewis "an elixir—true dimensions if a restricting scale." She must be careful not to "break his faith," she says, on the margin of this letter adding, "He has resources under and above and he's honest. If I can't transcend him, his ego can transcend me." To Dos Passos she laments that they "have not felt the same way at the same time," blaming "my initial error" and regretting he hadn't "wanted to come by me again." Before Christmas Dos wrote that he'd pass through Dallas on his way to Mexico. She introduced the men at the railroad station, and they seemed to approve of each other. A soliloquy after the novelist's visit clarifies the choice she is about to make:

> [Dos] is important to me, as a genre, as freedom, forever, the
> myth, the gleam, as simplicity and honesty. It was that ideal that

I subscribed to for four years, and complied with my father's, and soreness all around resulted. It is important to me that I'm important to Dos, because when once you have thought of anyone in one way, a way in which one can think of very few people in the world, one cannot be free of closeness to that person.

Now I'm in love with Lewis and Dos symbolizes an old allure and a present conviction—to whit simplicity, irresponsible simplicity. But that is because Lewis is caught and held, from his choice, in an environment that would circumscribe my external contacts [among other things, he occupied the top floor of his Victorian mother's home]. So Lewis, we have to work this out, being careful that I am not making a new pose. Do not reverence me, for that would be my disaster, for I am not worthy. What I want is for you to understand. When two people contract to live alongside, the essential is understanding, open understanding. I have got to be proud of myself, I have got never to regret how when I was free I disposed of my one life, because if one marries, although one can balance and with great skill preserve one's individuality, one can no longer utterly be free.

Lacking the millions James presents his heroine through Ralph Touchett, Crystal nonetheless refused the offer of a second year at SMU. "Dos has given me back myself, freed me from the five-foot shelf of books," she writes of what seems to have been advice against a career in general literature. She concludes, "Either of the three of us could go a separate way differently":

I do not honestly believe that I'm essential to Lewis in terms of life, or to Dos in terms of art. But enter my egotism: I should like to know which way my life will count for more. I am still free enough to make a go of anything, still young enough to make everybody see my way. Strange that things are so unhinged—if I had to choose what I elect to think is most important I could this minute flop either way and I could abide my choice and be careful not to regret either world, and

I could keep my soul for myself. But I don't want to keep my soul, I want to share my soul with Lewis if he can understand.

In terms of me, I know Lewis is more important. I want to think what is important in terms of art is not incompatible with what is true in terms of me. The fine arts are: sculpture, painting, music, literature, and life. It is fairly clear that whatever my little talents, my major one is for life—living—and that for the development of that talent, although Dos the symbol is a flaming inspiration, he is an intermittent inspiration, while Lewis is both an intermittent inspiration and a constant necessity—or does necessity carry constancy in its definition?

I insist that Lewis realize that I have gone through arriving, and that if he does not understand, if he does not see things as they are, that I have come up out of Lockhart and have been through Spain along the way, he must of course withdraw his support. We must be as we are but we have to find out who we are before we say to each other that we will play utterly together for awhile in this moving picture.

Little knowing what he had taken from his daughter, Doctor Ross saw this her second engagement as vindication. Crystal would often visit him in Lockhart, buoyed as children can be by slipping back into their pasts. All her life she subscribed to the *Lockhart Post-Register,* piling up the copies in closets and boxes. Yet she would build that life around Lewis Dabney, a more engaged lover than Dos and more tractable member of the patriarchy than her father. It was hard to let Dos go, and an April letter protests: "Of course I love you. I always have I always will. Innately I know I match you and anything that contradicts that suggests an unpleasant atrophy." As a June wedding looms her resolution wavers: "I felt clean-cut, and free to complete something once, until this ring appeared and Dallas without vacations loomed and every sunrise across White Rock [in the fashionable community of Highland Park, where Lewis and she would buy a lot] and me such a citizen of the world! And you out of the picture." She is going to marry Lewis, she says, but in theory can do anything when her SMU contract ends June 1. She can "step out from under and ease Eastward in the blue motor." It seems that diving into the ritual of the not yet known, that is, marriage, gave her the jitters.

In his first honest communication since her return to Texas Dos doesn't want her to make a mistake:

4/16/27

Dear Crys,

I've been back about a month, involved in a theatre that is starting jerkily painfully and with infinites of 20–25 hour a day work. It's the night of the full moon and it's spring. I'm beastly lonely in my room above the steamboat whistles and I've just reread your letter.

He tiptoes up to the possibility of changing course:

Crys, old kid, don't get married unless you're crazy about the guy. The day I saw him, he seemed to be an awfully good fellow. If you're crazy about him, forget everything and throw yourself at him. All this living with reservations is horrible. You've done too much of it and I've done too much of it. If you're not crazy about him, just hold your horses. Will you do that for me Crys? Honestly I like you much more and much less than I sometimes made you feel. But please Crys, if there are any reservations don't get married yet. If you still like me, I can get you over that—and then you can go ahead with a clear conscience. If I'd only known the stuff I know now about people that time we had no honeymoon in Holland, we'd both of us be much happier. Crys, if you're not absolutely crazy about him, drop me a line—I'll meet you anywhere anytime. At least we can have a talk. If you are crazy about him, tell me to go to hell. This may seem melodramatic and all that, but honestly everything gets so horrible if you don't make arbitrary distinctions. And remember Crys, that I can't promise a goddamn thing about how I'll feel or how you'll feel for a week, a month, a year, or a century.

How about it Crys? I've been meaning to write you this letter all winter but it never seemed to quite flow from the pen. Love Dos

110 Columbia Heights BKLN

He might have added, "Let's spend two weeks together and then each decide," but Crystal has scared him off, and he has let her down. In later life she would sometimes advise one to be arbitrary, and she was now. In June 1927 she and Lewis were married in the Episcopal chapel in Austin that had been a storage place for ammunition in the Civil War. They honeymooned in Mexico City.

Dos Passos stayed in touch. In October '27 he phoned from Massachusetts when arrested for picketing the Boston State House. Leading the protest against the executions of Sacco and Vanzetti after their widely disputed convictions for murder, he anticipated the leftward movement of artists and intellectuals after the Crash. When he visited the Soviet Union in 1928, he met Vsevolod Meyerhold, the stage director, and Sergei Eisenstein, whose films, like the cubist painters and the novels of Jules Romains, influenced Dos's cutback collage and speed techniques. A letter to Crystal is excited by the Moscow stage. Though the plays were "sometimes terrible," Russia was "a bath of energy for sick wills from the West." Dos was no potential Stalinist. He had heard the fear in the voice of an English Communist who witnessed the Cheka's brutal suppression of the Kronstadt sailors. Having finally made his way to Marx, he told Crystal he was surprised to find *Das Kapital* "magnificent reading."

He asked for one of her letters where competing subjects were harmonized, and she began with thrilling rides in the mountains above Santa Fe—"the only country, empty, barren, cruel, unbelievably beautiful." To her grandson she would recall the majesty of Holy Ghost Canyon, near the Pecos River going west. Perhaps it was there that she and a man from Chicago had been lost for hours and, as she wrote to Dos, "with tired unpredictable horses came at sunset to an open grave and followed the tracks to Indians." Less dramatic but vivid in the telling was a camping trip with Lewis in Canada "where the soft gentle opal make-your-own-adjective amethyst country is incisive with cold water." Exploring seven lakes and four creeks in abandoned logging country, they saw a variety of wildlife, which she lists, and "lived on cheese, bacon, bread and Scotch." She doesn't mention that she carried the canoe, while my father (later enjoying the joke on himself) cheered her on with, "Hurrah, boys, I've got the paddles!"

Dos Passos's male friends thought him subject to vagaries and doubts, a lack of nerve with women. He had overcome that with Crystal in Spain and in his quixotic effort to join her in Paris, but he hadn't tried to take on Lockhart without money, a wedding date, or evidence she could separate from her family. In the fall of 1929 he wrote to her that he had "fallen in love again and this time had it blessed by church and state." Kate Smith—like Betty Holdridge, whom he would marry after Kate's tragic death two decades later—was from a milieu where Dos was comfortable. The older sister of Hemingway's alcoholic fishing buddy Bill, whom Crystal met in Paris in 1925, they were children of a mathematician turned philosopher and biblical scholar. The Smiths had a house at the Cape where artists and writers got along on little money. There called Katy, she was one of the gang, writing magazine articles and collaborating on projects with Edie Shay, who lived next door and whose husband, Frank, owned the Provincetown bookstore. Unlike Hemingway's sister Marcelline, whom he couldn't interest in Dos, Katy was in a position to pursue the novelist and not too proud to do so. He was charmed by her eyes, calling them green, though others thought them yellow. Ross H. Dabney, my brother, remembered meeting Katy Dos Passos when they visited and he was eight or nine: "She had very large, light, blue-grey eyes." When Dos had gone off to start *The 42nd Parallel,* the first book of *U.S.A.,* she wrote hoping he wouldn't mind her letters, because "Love must have its say." She claimed her identity in naming it: "Do write me, darling, and tell me you miss your girl goil gerl gurl gal gurrl Katy."

On a driving trip with Bill Smith and Edith Foley, the couple got married, "taking out a license for one dollar in Ellsworth, Maine, and submitting to the ministrations of a slightly used Unitarian minister," Dos reported to Crystal. He split his pants and borrowed a raincoat to be married in. Bill let Katy have his share of the house on the harbor in Provincetown, and Dos bought a small farm in the hollow between the ponds in Truro, where he could grow vegetables. In a Christmas 1929 letter to Crystal, whom he'd advised not to marry unless crazy about Lewis, he declared himself "mad about Kate Smith." She replied: "Hooray for Kate Smith. I love you very much and I'm a fool about Kate Smith too, even as and because you are." She wished the two were with her—"I'm thinking you have the drop on the world, you do."

Dos was still a skittish bachelor in his rhetoric, to Wilson remarking that the organism of marriage "would take up as much room as it was allowed." A pert companion, Katy was six years older than he was and had had at least one miscarriage; she would be unable to have Dos's children as Crys had so wanted to do. She called on Crystal in Texas and then in Virginia, a few years later in Manhattan, questioning her "as if to find out my secret," my mother said. But Crystal knew that Dos's choice made sense if Katy cherished him. He found he cherished her, and she stabilized the life of the reporter-writer who came and went, always a rover.

C. R. D. on Hemingway and Others; Dos Passos's Women in *Manhattan Transfer* and *U.S.A.*

WHEN TOWNSEND LUDINGTON SET out to tell Dos Passos's story after his death in 1970, Ludington's student's encounter with my mother's niece led him to Crystal. Outlining their four years together from '23 to '27, she said nothing of her burst of critical writing after the thesis and before she married. But the "little talents" she dismissed in choosing Lewis ("life") over Dos ("art") included the gift, not visible in her dissertation, that makes her reviews of Hemingway in the *Dallas News* remarkable. It had contributed to Dos's wish that she were out of Strasbourg and beside him as he struggled with *Manhattan Transfer* in Brooklyn Heights.

Sketching Hemingway in his Parisian scene, her 1927 review locates the "brilliant hardness" of *The Sun Also Rises,* its "sustained tension," in the prose he'd helped create from the American vernacular. "Natural, vigorous, alive, direct," it conveyed essentials with superb economy and "an uncommon delicacy in omitting detail, in clipping off edges without marring contours or content." Looking back on the summer pilgrimage to Pamplona, Crystal finds "the sweetness and gaiety and courage and numb endurance" of these "in literary terminology disillusioned expatriates" less compelling than the prose that registered a new pulse in American life. She speaks for readers who, seeing themselves "in the speech and mannerisms of Hemingway's characters," rejoice "in the vicarious expression his art permits them." An aside calls *In Our Time* a distillation of the mind that created this way of writing: "The stories are hard to the point of cruelty; they are terrible and beautiful. This novel is neither; it is forthright, actual, and fine. It has the unbounded vigor and crisp accuracy of the stories, but not the enthusiasm that, repressed and controlled, characterized them." She is both accurate and subtle. Neither Wilson nor anyone else wrote so incisively of Hemingway's first triumphs.

Confirming that the country girl (as my father would christen her) had the gift of telling chalk from cheese, Crystal called attention to Faulkner's New Orleans satire *Mosquitoes* in an editorial column that spring, and in the fall she gave *Men without Women* an extraordinary review, a match for those of D. H. Lawrence and Virginia Woolf. The bride writing for regional readers on the top floor of her mother-in-law's house had absorbed enough of the great world of art and thought to see Hemingway at his best in "Indian Camp," "Hills Like White Elephants," "A Clean Well-Lighted Place": "The originality, the fidelity, the dramatic vigor, the studied-to-perfect simplicity of these stories proves Hemingway's astounding power in our time, and in all times when people shall be sensitive to colloquial art. For in his writing, the emotional and the intellectual join in a curious colloquial union; and in this union, those elements we called intellectual betray a subtle technical skill, and what we called emotion reveals a delicate forever-half-hidden spirituality; and this, through Hemingway's medium of stripped prose, is startling." Here Crystal, whose impressionism echoes the forms of university lecturing at Columbia and in France, saw that "the hardness and clarity of Hemingway's mind" made visual distinctions: "We are reminded of translucent geometrical screens in black frames, or white or gray, through which we observe brilliant colors just beginning to fade (for Hemingway seems to feel that illusion does not persist, that presently the bravest sail spills its wind)." His sentences were studied "to the least comma," as if the photographer "were very tightly holding together a particularly small camera, as he takes his picture." He was a realist in reportorial fiction, as Dos Passos was:

> But if this label is applied to John Dos Passos with his uncanny receiving and recording of detail, his use of all his faculties as reporting functions, it is not true of Hemingway. Nor is he objective in that way Flaubert sought to teach Maupassant, that he might look at any tree until that tree was different than all others and then explain this difference. Hemingway is objective in that he is dispassionate; he is even objective in the first person. And he is this kind of superb reporter: his exterior experience of life has been uncommonly varied and interesting and through an inner process, call it mental, emotional, artistic, he has boiled down certain of his experiences and observations and presented them in a deliberate art, so perfected as to seem an eighth wisdom, adapted to whosoever will.

With her dissertation behind her, Crystal could contrast this American to the Frenchman who held a "cold mirror" up to "hopeless reality." "With all his reportorial lucidity," she judged, "[Maupassant] was mad and himself escaped from that cruel mirror only into the raving freedom of a straightjacket." Thirty-three years before Hemingway chose suicide when threatened by madness, she saw the weight of depression in his work and confidently put it into words: "You turn from his polite, sane mirror having glimpsed planes of bitterness and wistfulness and charm and desperation and childlike gentleness that it is given average people rarely to feel, and, feeling, to recognize. He has, too, we feel, ineluctable proofs of the eternal, universal, indestructible and omnipotent stupidity, even cupidity, of the human race. But in spite of this and in a tone incessantly detached, he shows us compensation for the misery he sees and knows, in the elixir of sheer sport, and in the sweetness of sheer friendship."

Touching in its sensitivity, this reading of Hemingway, published in Dallas on return from her honeymoon, would help Crystal accommodate the dark aspect of his break with Dos over the Spanish Civil War. The two men, neither of whom seems to have known of these reviews, would have read them, each encouraging her as a critic and promoting her with editors. Here is where Crystal, compensating for what she harshly judged her dissertation's failure, achieves "the sweet bye and bye of being even with the world" which she'd liked to think Dos Passos "was rushing me toward." She had told her family she would support herself under her own name, C. R. R., but the initials would be "C. R. D." The second piece is signed Crystal Ross Dabney.

Though she wrote nothing about Dos's series of novels and chronicles, her mind and wit made their mark on the first of these, *Manhattan Transfer* (1925). He began the book in Paris after answering a pile of letters while awaiting money for the London trip. On a rainy day at the Hemingways he wrote to her of the grainy "roadhouse scene" that features a fight between rival gangs of bootleggers and would find its place in section 3. The book exemplifies the tenderness to which Dos had eagerly exposed her in Paris. Until the Moscow Trials of '36 and '38, artists found such an aesthetic compatible with revolutionary politics. At his perch above the harbor in Brooklyn Heights, a step removed from the turbulence across the river, Dos Passos worked from story to novel as Hemingway did, but with different priorities, creating a personal voice from what he'd heard in gatherings and on the streets. *Manhattan Transfer* incorporates newspaper headlines and text, song lyrics, a scene or two in a play. It moves toward the formally divided perspective of *U.S.A.*, where ordinary lives are played off against the jazzy satire of the newsreels, compressed biographies of influential Americans, the autobiographical vignettes of the "Camera Eye." Dos's book is part of the current running from *Winesburg, Ohio,* Joyce's *Dubliners,* and Gertrude Stein to Faulkner's gothic novels of isolation and community in the South of the thirties. Twenties New York is the protagonist of *Manhattan Transfer.* Sex, money and career are the plot, marriage involving all three. People turn up in each other's lives in a collage of overlapping tales without interiority or backstory, of scenes that are darkly energetic, even apocalyptic. The nerve of the book jumps just beneath the skin.

Edmund Wilson's journal records escaping from a Princeton football game at the last reunion he attended into his friend's re-creation in *Manhattan Transfer* of American speech during their boyhood. Jimmy Herf, whose adolescent summers on the Potomac were Dos Passos's subject in the *Transatlantic Review,* here becomes a New Yorker and reporter for the *New York Times* as Wright McCormick had been. Dos amalgamates memories of his mother, her illness and death, with satirical sketches of his relatives on Riverside Drive. Jimmy's vis-à-vis is Ellen Thatcher, actress daughter of a struggling accountant. Ellen first marries John Oglethorpe, finding protection in an older man who is gay and a theater buff. She will briefly acquire a husband along with her son, as shy Dos had imagined achieving a family the easy way with Kate Drain. Other players are introduced: George Baldwin, a lawyer, gets his foot on the success ladder as an ambulance chaser, winning a ten-thousand-dollar verdict for the injured wagon-driver Gus McNeil while seducing his wife, with whom he briefly is in love. After Gus becomes a leader of the labor movement, the dreadful Baldwin enters New York politics as a reformer. Two French-speaking immigrants are Herf's friends as the book opens and closes. Emile, a decent enough scalawag, finds his place by marrying a fat female butcher whose dead husband was also named Emile. The mulatto Congo Jake, a drifter turned successful bootlegger, renames himself Armand Duval and moves to Park Avenue, where he hears Jimmy mull over his life before leaving town.

Bud Korpenning's story leads the reader to the Brooklyn Bridge as the Whitmanesque aspect of *Manhattan Transfer* unfolds in section 1. Both Dos and the poet Hart Crane, his neighbor at Columbia Heights, were drawn to the aspiration of the bridge and to its dark shadow:

> How many dawns, chill from his rippling rest
> The seagull's wings shall dip and pivot him,

C. R. D. on Hemingway; Dos Passos's Women

Shedding white rings of tumult, building high
Over the chained bay waters Liberty—

So begins Crane's lofty "Proem: To Brooklyn Bridge," only to conclude in discouraged January:

Under thy shadow by the piers I waited;
Only in darkness is thy shadow clear.
The City's fiery parcels all undone,
Already snow submerges an iron year . . .

Bud, Dos's gloomy hero—who has an alternate, glamorously success-ful self in his head—is on the lam from a farmer's life in upstate New York, after killing the abusive father who regularly beat him with a chain. Always homeless, ever afraid of the police, he gets fifty cents for what turns out to be a last supper from a bum in whom he confides of the money he'd buried at home. The sun rises over the blue night as the fugitive picks his teeth and climbs the edifice before him: "When he got to the tangle of girders of the elevated railroads on the Brooklyn side, he turned back along the southern driveway. Don't matter where I go, can't go nowhere now. All the darkness was growing pearly, warming. They're all of them detectives, chasin' me all of them. Old women in kitchens, barkeeps, streetcar conductors, bulls, hookers, sailors, longshoremen, stiffs in employment agencies. Mists fringed the river; smoke, purple space, chocolatecolor, fleshpink, climbed into light. Can't go nowhere now." Whitman is reversed, the categories and classes of people not all brothers but one's enemies. Sitting on the rail as Manhattan's windows catch fire, Korpenning summons the courage to let go, the yell strangling in his throat as he drops. Ten years after Dos's novel appeared and five after the publication of Crane's poem, the poet jumped to his death from the stern of a tramp steamer.

In the section 2 of *Manhattan Transfer*, writing with Crystal in her own struggle an ocean away, Dos attunes himself to gritty women of his acquaintance who, with little social power and a justified fear of pregnancy, had to negotiate their lives through men. Consider Cassie, the lost soul who turns to Ellen for help with an abortion, or the unnamed character who, in the last sentence of section 2, climbs off the abortionist's table and orders a cab "to the Ritz." While married to Oglethorpe, Ellen falls passionately in love with alcoholic Harvard playboy Stanwood Emery and becomes pregnant. Stan spends a weekend at Niagara Falls with a pickup named Pearline and wakes up married to her, then sets his New York apartment and himself afire. Thus does Dos Passos elaborate on the melodrama of Fitzgerald's "May Day" (1922), where the bride is named Jewel and the hero shoots himself in the head in his hotel room. While Pearline shrieks over the loss of "my husband Stanwood," Ellen resolves to put aside a silly life and bring up the child, moving Herf to propose marriage. But the bloom is off the rose when they return from France with the baby at the beginning of section 3. At first a househusband, Jimmy is maneuvered out of the house after he agrees to keep a separate room for his writing. Emotionally burned out, Ellen divorces him to make her cynical marriage to Baldwin, who is getting rid of his wife and can use a trophy beside him when he runs for mayor.

References to World War I set off the downward swirl of personalities and tales in the novel's last chapters. A version of the Triangle Fire horrifically maims a young woman in a clothing sweatshop, a scene like that which influenced young Frances Perkins, whom FDR would make his first secretary of labor. A couple with no money become criminals, are caught, and the man, Jake Silverman, receives a long sentence. When carted off to jail, Jake leaves Rosie a note marked by Dos's generous instinct: "Hock everything and beat it; you're a good kid." He never says life is ugly, but it is. The novelist whose parties quite lack the gaiety of Gatsby's can't wait for the Jazz Age to end:

> [Jimmy Herf] sat in Washington Square, pink with noon, looking up Fifth Avenue through the arch. The fever had seeped out of him. He felt cool and tired. In Yonkers I buried my childhood, in Marseilles with the wind in my face I dumped my calf years into the harbor.

C. R. D. on Hemingway; Dos Passos's Women

Where in New York shall I bury my twenties? Maybe they were deported and went out to sea on the Ellis Island ferry singing the Internationale.

DEPORTED

James Herf, young newspaperman of 190 West 12th Street, recently lost his twenties. Appearing before Judge Merivale [named for one of Dos's New York relatives] they were remanded to Ellis Island for deportation as undesirable aliens. The younger four Sasha Michael Nicholas and Vladimir had been held for some time on a charge of criminal anarchy. . . . All were convicted on counts of misfeasance, malfeasance, and nonfeasance.

It turns out that everyone is too drunk for the trial to go on. When *Manhattan Transfer* went to press in May '25, Dos Passos knew the radical avant-garde was breaking up in the crisis of capitalism, a subject that was clearer when Sacco and Vanzetti were executed in 1927.

The concluding conversation at Congo/Armand's Park Avenue apartment looks ahead to *Nineteen Nineteen* and *The Big Money*. Jimmy denounces Ellen's heartlessness in the manner of a man who knows he has failed with women: "Women are like rats you know, they leave a sinking ship. She's going to marry this man Baldwin who's just been appointed District Attorney. The delusion of power, that's what's biting him. Women fall for it like hell." He insists he has lost such interest as he ever had in money and social position. As Congo listens "with his heavy lips a little open," Jimmy, on his third glass of bourbon, declares: "If I thought it'd be any good to me I swear I've got the energy to sit up and make a million dollars. But I get no organic sensation out of that stuff any more. I've got to have something new, different. Your sons'll be like that, Congo. But here I am by Jesus Christ almost thirty years old and very anxious to live." In the colonnaded hall as he leaves the building, soon to hitchhike out of NYC, Jimmy runs into another old friend. Nevada Jones says she has lost her job as Baldwin's mistress because she was sleeping with Tony Hunter, a closeted homosexual out to cure himself, "afraid he was going to be unfaithful to me with an acrobat." In the meantime Nevada and Congo have found each other. They're happily married, happy too with their new cook, Emile. It's the tidying up that ends a classical comedy, although the union of the principal parties ended in divorce, and the author, clearly, is not ready to marry.

For Fitzgerald, *Manhattan Transfer* was astonishingly good in technique, for Sinclair Lewis perhaps "the foundation of a whole new school of novel writing." It was "a spiritual Baedeker to New York" for Hemingway; for Lawrence it caught "the vast shuffle of Manhattan Island, a very complex film of the loose gang of strivers, winners, and losers." Wilson, with high standards for his own fiction, judged the book not "free from rhetoric doing duty for feeling and from descriptions too relentlessly piled up." By decade's end he thought one should be able "to hold Dos Passos's political opinions and yet not depict our middle-class republic as a place where no birds sing, no flowers bloom, and where the very air is almost unbreathable." As if foreseeing Dos Passos's later chronicles, he proposed that "When so intelligent a man and so good an artist falsifies his picture to the point of melodrama," the reader can envision "some stubborn sentimentalism at the bottom of the whole thing." The novelist's political journey starts over at the end of *Manhattan Transfer,* when Herf the hitchhiker, asked how far he is going, answers, "Pretty far." His voice recurs in the populist, quasi-Marxist invocation to *The 42nd Parallel:* "U.S.A. is a set of big-mouthed officials with too many bank accounts. U.S.A. is a lot of men buried in their uniforms in Arlington Cemetery. U.S.A. is the letters at the end of an address when you are away from home. But mostly U.S.A. is the speech of the people." Herf is there, too, at the end of *The Big Money* and the trilogy, behind the mask of the tramp Vag, who "aches with wants" while a plane heads west toward Los Angeles many thousands of feet above him. It is Dos on the 1 percent and the 99:

> The transcontinental passenger thinks contracts, profits,
> vacationtrips, mighty continent between Atlantic and Pacific, power,
> wires humming dollars. . . .

C. R. D. on Hemingway; Dos Passos's Women

The young man waits on the side of the road; the plane has
gone. . . . Waits with swimming head, needs knot the belly, idle hands
numb, beside the speeding traffic.
A hundred miles down the road.

All this had a more radical vibration in the Soviet Union before the
Moscow trials, when modern American writers were fashionable.
During his months on the margin of Moscow in 1935, Wilson heard
dissident young Russians identify themselves as Jimmy Herf.

The take on sex, money, and power in *Manhattan Transfer* is extended in *U.S.A.*, where we sympathetically observe pressures on
women in a man's world. Eleanor Stoddard and Eveline Hutchins,
well-educated, articulate, and able, come east from Chicago together
to lead connected lives in the circle of J. Ward Morehouse, emerging
tycoon of K Street and Madison Ave. Each is drawn to what Herf, ob-
serving this ersatz patriarchy as Dos did, calls "the delusion of power."
In J. W.—who had wanted to be a songwriter—Dos Passos depicts a
modern American elite of influence peddlers, using the traits of the
once famous Ivy Lee, with whom he talked while Lee made strate-
gic connections in Moscow. Eveline scatters herself among men and
projects, as Eleanor succumbs to the sublimated power drive. The
third woman of *U.S.A.* is the Texan Anne Elizabeth Trent, who is a
diminished version of Crystal Ross, with Crystal's magnetism though
quite lacking her intellectual and moral authority. Anne Elizabeth is
referred to as Daughter by the other characters, as if it were her given
name. Tellingly, she is never shown oppressed by her father. Our honest
novelist roots his characters in what he knows, and instead of targeting
a stand-in for Dr. Ross, has left Daughter's tacit acquiescence to the
Texas patriarchy unexplained.

Traits and experiences in Crystal's early letters appear in the two
"Daughter" chapters that expand Dos's canvas into Texas. She has a
gun in her purse, is a swimmer prone to accidents, "picks up" a young
soldier at a railroad station, works out stress by playing sports with

her girlfriend, and so on. In *Nineteen Nineteen* and *The Big Money* her naivete, daring, and stubbornness are set among leftist labor agitators in New York and Paris rather than in the twenties of literary expatriates. Daughter makes a name for herself when enraged by police brutality to a woman striker ("Texas Belle Assaults Cop" is the headline). That her brother Bud is killed flying a defective plane in World War I gives her a cause, even as it gave Arthur Miller, who admired Dos, the plot of *All My Sons*. Sexually a neophyte just as Crystal was, Anne Elizabeth is undone when she moves from young radicals in wartime New York City to established careerists making connections in President Wilson's entourage for the Peace Conference.

She falls for Richard Ellsworth Savage, the cowardly villain who acquires J. W.'s power at the end of *U.S.A.* Savage is a cad, and Dos admits the possibility in himself. Of a family that once had money, fancying he may be a minor poet, he is a general's grandson, and on returning as Dos had from the elite Norton-Harjes Ambulance Service, is helped to a regular army commission. In Paris and Italy Dick is on the success ladder, doomed to be hollowed out like J. W. before him. Daughter gets pregnant, and Dick abandons her when her condition is clear. Alone in Paris and Rome (no power, no birth control), as her other male friends turn away and the Red Cross, for whom she works, prepares to send her home in disgrace, she finds herself in a dark corner of Dos's creative psychology. When I asked Mother how women of the twenties coped with the fear of pregnancy, she said they passed it on to their men in the form of guilt. Her grandiose request of him to fly a plane with her even if it is in "a tailspin over Mt. Sinai" is the climax of the pregnancy drama in *U.S.A.* Savage also bears Dos's uneasiness at having made no effort to rescue Crystal in Texas. Though the novelist, too, had deserted his girl, he hadn't first made her pregnant, nor did they take a pseudo-honeymoon that could have ended with "the shine of a wing gliding by itself a little way from the plane."

The fate that Daughter brings on herself and the innocent French aviator is coordinated with the draining of vitality and sympathy in the emerging capitalist bureaucracy seen taking over in *U.S.A.* The major woman in Savage's life is not Daughter but Eleanor Stoddard, who consoles herself by pouring tea for J. W. while obsessively focused (as Lear contemptuously has it) on "who's in, who's out." In *Nineteen Nineteen* she claims the seducer's role, insidiously telling Dick, "We might get J. W. to fix up something for you. How would you like to be one of his bright young men?": "She patted the back of his hand: 'That's what I like about you, Richard, the appetite you have for everything.... J. W. spoke several times about that keen look you have. He's like that, he's never lost his appetite, that's why he's getting to be a power in the world. You know Colonel House consults him all the time. You see, I've lost my appetite.' They went back to the tea-table." Eleanor's false characterization of J. W. as a winner evokes the Freudian exchange of eros for authority, redolent of the castration complex, reflecting Dos's enthusiastic letter to Crys about *The Interpretation of Dreams*. When Eleanor silkily apologizes for saying "An unsuitable marriage has been the ruination of many a promising young fellow," Dick responds, "I like you taking an interest like that, honestly it means a great deal to me" (thus does the fly relax into the spider's web). That night, having cut Anne Elizabeth loose, he thinks of her alone in Paris in "a hell of a rotten world." As he lies in bed, a Prufrockian figure "between the clammy sheets, his eyes [are] pinned open with safety pins," but when his feet warm up he falls comfortably asleep.

Savage appears at two trivial occasions in *Nineteen Nineteen*'s last pages. J. W. has a press conference about an international oil deal, involving American producers and Royal Dutch-Shell. Dick manages the public relations even as he absorbs Daughter's suicide, trying to keep the stories that contain his name out of the papers. The second occasion is Eleanor's wedding party for Eveline, who, back in New York, married because pregnant. Paul Johnson has behaved honorably; he apologizes for helping put her in this position. As gifts for Eleanor he and Eveline bring two parakeets, one of whom is dead at party's end. Four hundred pages later, Dick's fate rounds out *The Big Money* in a judgment on the new American culture. Beating out a rival, he becomes J. W.'s partner by capturing the big contract with a patent medicine producer, who gives them the account after Dick opens to him the fleshpots of New York. The country bumpkin's daughter is already established in a penthouse, and a pink, perfumed envelope from her invites Savage to a reception.

An artist's deepest record is his work, and these relationships show where Dos was psychologically and politically between Crystal's marriage in June 1927 and his own in August 1929. *U.S.A.*'s bitter conclusion is remote from *Manhattan Transfer*'s breezy one. Eveline Hutchins, with whom J. W. had a weekend fling in France and Italy at the time of the Versailles negotiations, asks him for a ten-thousand-dollar loan that would enable her to enlist the Shuberts' backing for a play she wants to produce. When the sympathetically inclined but physically collapsing tycoon runs her request past Savage, he gratuitously advises turning it down. Thus Dick kills his soul as Eleanor long since has hers.

At the very end of *The Big Money* we learn that Eveline ended her life with sleeping pills after a reception at which she announced that her play would not go on. The book's larger themes are the next morning addressed by Mary French, a labor organizer Dos admires, her politics indebted to the Provincetown radical journalist Mary Heaton Vorse. More important to French than Eveline's suicide is the loss of the truck driver murdered while courageously supplying the picket line. Mary has the Marxist morality that through the thirties held the left-wing culture of Dos Passos's generation together, as David Brooks puts it in a review (titled "The Big Money"). Brooks is skeptical of George Packer's brilliant *The Unwinding*, written in a journalistic tradition indebted to Dos Passos. Mary doesn't retreat when the man is shot, resolving to move her operation into the owners' territory. Although none of the cast in *U.S.A.* sees where the social machine is going, the reader correlates the fulfillment/frustration of these characters with the political history told in the newsreels and biographies. The durability of *U.S.A.* derives from these connections.

PART IV

The Unorthodox New Dealer
and the Unlikely Republican

CRYSTAL AND LEWIS LEARNED to "play utterly together for a while in this moving picture." Through the first seven years of his marriage Lewis worked in his father's and another Dallas law firm, and was toughened up in the oil fields. He wrote an article about the law's paradoxes for the *Southwest Review*. There were lawyers like Jack Hyman whom he loved. An unpleasant figure was Dick Knight, a lawyer's son who grew up across the street from Lewis, but in the eastern scene of Fitzgerald and Wilson acquired the reputation of a cad. Visiting Dallas, Knight made late-night phone calls to Crystal until her scrawny young husband, at a party on a top-floor deck, threatened to throw him off the building. For a while, Crys taught English at the Hockaday School for Girls, and in Dallas a constituency of young women looked to her for guidance. "We all sat at her feet," recalled "Billie" [Mrs. Stanley] Marcus. Fannie [Mrs. Adolph] Harris and her son Leon became lifelong friends, as were the architect O'Neil Ford and his colleague Dave Williams, a storytelling adventurer. This circle overlapped with the little theater group, including Crystal's baby sister, Zerilda, who came up from Lockhart. When they put on *Lady Windemere's Fan* Crys beat the drums in a piece on Wilde for the *News*. "Oscar Wilde undoubtedly had in him a spurt of divine fire, although he used it only in the pyrotechnics of paradox," she wrote, citing the epigraphs about criticism in *Intentions*. That Wilde should ever have found the Philistines "worth mystifying" was "the real tragedy." The Irish dramatist had chosen to be "the fop of genius," been "bunkoed into taking the propertied classes at their own valuation."

In the early thirties, future Supreme Court justice Felix Frankfurter began recommending Lewis to New Dealers. Fortunate in this fatherly interest, Lewis flirted with a job at the Tennessee Valley Authority (TVA). At Frankfurter's suggestion, in 1935 he joined the Securities and Exchange Commission in Washington as an assistant general counsel. The young couple moved north with their two sons, born in 1932 and 1934. After six months without, he recalled, anything much to do, he began a successful prosecution of Howard Hopson, whose public utility monopoly, Associated Gas and Electric, Alabama senator Hugo Black (appointed by Roosevelt to the Supreme Court in '37) had made emblematic of arrogant wrongdoing. The Texan eventually put Hopson in jail. In these middle years of the New Deal, Crystal and Lewis, living on Lee Street in Alexandria and in Fairfax County, met brilliant westerners and southerners. Their closest friends were an older couple, Judge Thurman Arnold, the Wyoming lawyer out of Yale who would found Arnold, Fortas, and Porter after he left the bench, and his wife, Frances, a Missourian. Crystal had no literary world as in Dallas, and her husband worked long hours, but on weekends there were bohemian parties. The guitar players included Mary Cabell Calloway, who ran a fabled summer camp on the James River (attended by my brother Ross and me), and Coleman Grey, who had come back from Dijon, France, with a doctorate in literature and the recipe for Grey's Poupon Mustard. Dabney learned to play the mandolin, could pick out "Waiting for the Robert E. Lee" on the tenor banjo.

It was fun being a youthful reformer, he recalled. But he wasn't an orthodox New Dealer, and during the Popular Front of the late thirties grew unhappy with the Stalinist line promoted on the left as an answer to Hitler. Judge Arnold recalled that Lewis "had too much political courage." Arnold sketched the evening when all the young lawyers were given a minute or two apiece to share their concerns with Eleanor Roosevelt, whose entourage famously turned out to have included Communists. They were encouraged to tell her what was on their minds. The next man ascending the stage heard Dabney first compliment some of Mrs. R's social policies, then state that in his opinion "the primary difference between Germany and Russia is it's colder in Russia." Dos Passos, too, was a contrarian. *The 42nd Parallel,* published as the decade began, confirmed his place among leaders of the American literary Left. Now the Communists promoted him as America's "leading proletarian writer," while he saw the Russian Revolution sliding into Stalin's terror, as did European radicals like Orwell, Silone, Malraux, and Koestler. His friend Wilson, then writing *To the Finland Station,* endorsed Marxist socialism but dismissed the American Communist Party and went to see Russia for himself in 1934, six years after Dos Passos's 1928 trip.

In 1936 Hemingway signed on with the Republican revolution in Spain, a country to which he was romantically attached, and the Spanish Civil War changed the relationship of these two even as it redirected Dos's politics. As the Moscow trials began in 1936, Dos went to Spain intending to resume work on the film *The Spanish Earth,* to which Hemingway and others contributed. He was also determined to look into the disappearance of his old friend Jose Robles, whom he'd seen more of when hospitalized with rheumatic fever in Baltimore. As aide to Ivan Gorev, commander of the Soviet military police in Spain, Robles had been imprudent. He had tried to persuade an imprisoned reactionary brother, once an aide to the king, to switch sides and may have discussed military strategy at a café. At the end of '36 he was advised that he would be wise to leave the country, but he didn't do so as Madrid's citizens surprisingly fought off Franco's advance. He became victim of a "special section" of police under control of the NKVD. Carried away in the night by men who didn't identify themselves and made no charges, he was executed in late February or March 1937, as Stalin broke the back of the Spanish anarchists and labor unions. The foreign minister of the Republic repeatedly lied to Dos, not even providing a promised death certificate so that the man's penniless family could collect his American insurance. Andres Nin, once Trotsky's secretary, who headed the POUM militia Orwell saw suppressed in Barcelona, was murdered not long after Dos Passos interviewed him about his experiences. The Russian for whom Robles worked was sent home to be feted at the Kremlin and disposed of two days later.

Though the opening up of the Soviet archives after the fall of communism would yield no revelations about Robles or his Russian boss, in the fine book *The Breaking Point: Hemingway, Dos Passos, and the Murder of Jose Robles* (2005), Stephen Koch portrays the young Dutch filmmaker Jorge Ivens, a student of Eisenstein whom Dos took on to coordinate *The Spanish Earth,* directing the Soviet propaganda push. Ivens made the most of Dos's idealistic naivete and Hemingway's predilection for belittling perceived rivals. Hemingway was led to announce to Dos Passos, without evidence and at a public meeting, that Robles had been executed "as a traitor." He was soon saying that Dos— who had never shared Hemingway's interest in blood sports—was a coward, perhaps treacherous. By the end of the grim Spanish Civil War, Dos Passos had lost control of his film and hated the Kremlin and its apologists. *For Whom the Bell Tolls* made Hemingway the new Popular Front favorite—the anti-Stalinist *Partisan Review* cleverly called this "Substitution at Left Tackle." The signing of the Nazi-Soviet Pact on August 23, 1939, sealed the literary Left's disillusionment. The friendship of John Dos Passos and Ernest Hemingway was done.

There are traces of the troubling themes of betrayal and exposure in four of Hemingway's Spanish war stories, "The Denunciation," "The Butterfly and the Tank," "Night before Battle," and "Under the Ridge," all written during his work on *For Whom the Bell Tolls*. The author swallows his own propaganda in the self-indulgent play *The Fifth Column,* whose hero fulfills the appetites of the Vassar girl in his tent when not at the dark task of bagging Fascist spies and sympathizers. But in the novel completed after Franco won the war, he has largely sloughed off his Stalinism in a story of life and death among guerrillas on a mountaintop, with a subplot romance, and including memorable vignettes of the wartime cruelty of both Fascists and Republicans. The novel uses versions of Jung's archetypes—earth mother Pilar, weak father Pablo, virginal sister-lover Maria, all setting off Jordan, the hero whose victory is his necessary sacrifice.

Dos Passos's literary response to the war was *Adventures of a Young Man,* which ends when his protagonist, an ex–New Dealer turned independent radical, is sent out by Communist authorities to be killed by the Fascists. Soon after it appeared, Malcolm Cowley reviewed the novel in the July 1939 *New Republic.* Illustrating a penchant of literary radicals, Cowley, then a Communist, had less to say of the book than of its politics and turned to personalities, comparing Dos Passos's supposed confusion to Hemingway's clarity about Robles's guilt. In a letter to Cowley, Wilson denounced his old protégé as a Stalinist hack. Yet without Cowley's review we wouldn't have Dos Passos's reasoned, restrained, at points icy protest to the magazine or the information revealed there (appendix C). Calling Robles's fate "one story among thousands in the vast butchery that was the Spanish Civil War," Dos says it offers "a glimpse into the bloody tangle of ruined lives that underlay the hurray for our side aspects."

Crystal may have seen this letter, since she read the old *New Republic,* the most literary of political weeklies when Wilson helped direct its course from 1925 through the end of the thirties. She bought all Dos's novels and read *Adventures of a Young Man.* She knew his rationality and ability to control his ego, also that Hemingway was shaky—didn't need to observe his sycophants in later years to know what the friendship of equal figures had meant for both. After she took her boys by train from Texas to Washington, DC, she joined the two novelists in what may have been their last genial encounter. They met at Stratford, Robert E. Lee's family home a few miles from Spence's Point. She brought along the present writer, apparently to show me off.

World War II would make Washington the most powerful place in the world, but in 1940 Lewis Dabney began practicing law in New York, where, as trustee of Associated Gas, he saw the corporation into and through bankruptcy, twice pursuing Howard Hopson into prison—paradoxically, Hopson, who used his mental health as a "Get Out of Jail Free" card, died in an asylum. In Dabney's later years he pioneered in what would be a new kind of securities law, bringing stockholders' suits against such corporate giants as Chase, Kaiser-Frazer, and Chrysler. Crystal and Lewis had no equivalent of their young professionals in Dallas, the Brain Trust acquaintances they met in Washington, or the easygoing crowd in Alexandria, but she loved New York's anonymity and sophistication.

Through the forties the family owned a townhouse on Manhattan's Upper East Side (175 E. Eightieth Street, between Lexington and Third Avenue). It wasn't a conventional establishment. One of the bedrooms on the fourth floor was occupied by our butler, William Colbert, a flashy character with Harlem connections, who kept the Dabney boys in line, offering—or threatening, when we invaded his domain via the dumb waiter shaft—to make us an Uptown Zombie. William had Saturday-night parties for homosexual friends in our large kitchen, and they and we all got in trouble when he showed off Crystal's pistol to such a gathering. Arrested for violating the Sullivan Act, my mother was taken downtown in the middle of the night, but Father somehow got her off. The other fourth-floor room belonged to Parker, a Black Virginian Mother was teaching to read and write, who apparently had a job somewhere else. German Yorkville during World War II could be an uneasy place to live. A 2013 New Yorker cover on which a blonde woman in bed with her laptop and cell phone is terrified by a huge Uncle Sam, the peeping-and-listening Tom at her bedroom window, takes me back to a childhood image of Sam looming down from the several-story side of Hans Jæger's restaurant on Eighty-Sixth Street, his words a warning to all but himself: "Be careful. Enemy ears may be listening."

Crystal was lonely after 1948, with my brother and I at boarding school and then college, and she fell into drinking by herself at home. Throughout her middle years she struggled to accept that she was an alcoholic, and that her determined moral will didn't change this. Lewis was her codependent, not a binge drinker as my mother sometimes was but one who could drink steadily from noon into the night, without its apparently ever affecting his practice of law. In her ongoing crisis Crystal was guided by a psychoanalyst who encouraged self-study. Needing occupation, for years she was devoted to the Yorkville Youth Council. During Stevenson's second run for the presidency in 1956 she led his Volunteers in Manhattan, working under Senator Albert Gore Sr., who recalled all this fifty years later. In penciled notes found among Crystal's papers she is stimulated by a Victorian poetry anthology to set down qualities of Arnold's verse—"calm contemplation, not urgent but with an imperative impulse"—a "real interest in life and thought," the verse "fresh, pellucid, mannered." In his prose she sees "the freedom of the liberated spirit." But as a New York woman at midcentury, she lacked the outlet for literary criticism which a regional newspaper had afforded. It was apparently through Elizabeth (Babs) Janeway and her husband, Eliot, a political operator (they acquired a showplace on E. Eightieth Street at Fifth Avenue when they moved from Washington to New York) that Crys was asked to review films for the new magazine *Cue*. It was a chance to do substantive work. If she had joined her dead-on accuracy and high seriousness as a reviewer, bringing an eye and ear developed through literature to a related art and its language, Crystal might have achieved a deeper investment of herself in New York. Unfortunately, Lewis, though he always admired his wife's voice on the page, discouraged her from what he thought an unnecessary job. It was a conventional husbandly response at the time.

She found an answer of sorts when they moved halfway back to the South in 1950, acquiring a farm on Maryland's Eastern Shore where the family came to spend much of the year. She'd talked of always wanting "to keep house for a colony—on the side—in just such an adequate, selfless way," as she put it to Dos when they first knew each other. At Pickbourn on Miles River Neck she achieved this around the clock, providing a refuge for Washington friends while endlessly nursing the box bushes, escaping in necessary retreats to the *pied-a-terre* that had been the library of a building designed by Stanford White and that when sold, succeeded our New York house.

Her life and Dos's now ran parallel. In 1943–44, he prevailed in the courts over the relatives who had at best mismanaged his Virginia property, and when in 1948 he and his half brother Louis were able to divide the land they inherited, he acquired 2,100 acres including the more valuable Potomac waterfront. Katy and he began trying to get the house they liked at Spence's Point in order. Dos Passos had sometimes likened himself to an ape and Katy to a possum. The woman who had been his "girl goil gurl gal gurrl" now marketed herself as "Passionately devoted/Eternally faithful/Bookkeeping/Bookwriting/Painting/Cleaning working/In the garden furbishing/Architectural/agricultural" Katy Dos Possum. Owning up to one sin, she here adds to her list of attributes "monetary"—a trait that Hemingway, with his competitive asperity, now associated with Katy and Dos.

The gulf between Dos Passos's early and his later work involves a personal transformation that matched the ideological one accomplished by Spain and World War II, with the backing of newly felt Virginia roots. His life was catastrophically broken in the September 1947 car crash that killed Katy and cost Dos the sight of his right eye. Momentarily blinded by the setting sun on a Massachusetts highway near Provincetown, Dos ran into the back of a truck with its tailgate down. The top of their car was sheared off, and Katy "practically decapitated." Behaving with courage and a sense of responsibility to his "lost love," Dos, hospitalized through the funeral (a well-known letter from Edmund Wilson filled him in), found he couldn't stand living at the Cape without his companion of two decades. In 1950, the year that the Dabneys bought Pickbourn on Maryland's Eastern Shore, he began over in Virginia with Elizabeth (Betty) Holdridge, whose first husband, an explorer of the Amazon-Orinoco watershed, had "been killed in an auto accident at about the time that Katy was killed," Dos wrote to Crystal.

Betty, too, was a responsive woman from a milieu where he was comfortable, someone who could gently take the lead. He met her through Lloyd and Marian Lowndes, whose home in Sneden's Landing on the Hudson north of New York City (not far from Gerald and Sara Murphy's) was a refuge for him after Katy's death. Betty was tall and attractive, with a reserved manner and quiet humor. Dos seemed to her "lonely, distracted, even disoriented," as she had been when her husband, Desmond Holdridge, and Marian Lowndes's brother Emerson were killed together. Dos Passos and she had one or two lunch dates, and on a Memorial Day weekend the Smith graduate, then working in the art department at *Reader's Digest,* helped him organize some articles about the wheat business for General Mills. He invited her to dinner before he put her on the train. "As they sat conversing," she recalled to Townsend Ludington, "she reached to pick up something on the table and he leaned over and put his hand on hers. 'Well,' Dos asked, 'Is it one for all and all for one?'" She realized this hesitant, good man was asking her to marry him and she said yes. They were married at her brother-in-law's farm north of Baltimore. Betty and he finished fixing up the Virginia house, and they soon delighted Crystal by having a child they could name Lucy for Dos's mother.

Betty was not threatened by Crystal as Katy appears to have been, and Dos and she saw each other again in New York. At the New York apartment she named the Reading Room, she showed him the Murphy beds she'd had built in behind the library bookshelves for her two sons, each six feet tall ("they're good-and-long beds—a feat"). Afterward she wrote to Dos, perhaps the only person with whom she discussed the boys' combativeness, that she brought Lewis and Ross together there "to try to illumine some of the sources of their bias and insecurity, to the purpose of adult self-orientation and, or, of expiating parental liabilities of com and omission" (appendix D). In the country Dos and she sometimes felt connected by the Chesapeake Bay watershed, but they were so far apart by car, on different sides of both the Chesapeake and the Potomac, that he thought they should visit each other by helicopter. As a gentleman farmer Dos led a new kind of life, personally happier perhaps than any time since "the great days" of 1923–28, as they are called in *The Best Times*. When Edmund Wilson visited him in Virginia, Dos said that to accommodate a farmer's duties he did much of his writing before nine in the morning. He had pretensions as a country squire (just as Wilson did), but my father won the title, for he was nominated and crowned by his wife. She refers to him as the Squire in her 1957 letter to Dos, while cataloging her versatility at country tasks. This letter hopes they'll visit back and forth. After describing a crowded Easter weekend at Pickbourn, she runs through a delicious day of "reforms and remedies that are rewarding in the *very* early spring." Adding ten lines at the mailbox, she signs off, "heady with tranquility, solitude and silence."

Dos's quasi-baronial heritage came too late in life to change a loner's instincts, but it gave him a certain weight as an American democrat in *The Ground We Stand On* (1941) and *The Head and Heart of Thomas Jefferson* (1954). The latter book, "with its conversation between Jefferson's head and heart," reminds me of my father's capacity, as my brother says, to patronize Jefferson. Dos's other books variously join social history to personal chronicle, including *Mr. Wilson's War,* an important time for him. A second trilogy, focused on the District of Columbia, begins with *Adventures of a Young Man* and includes *Number One* (ostensibly about Huey Long) and *The Grand Design*. A sustained attack on bureaucratic power in the name of American freedom, it is usually considered opinionated rather than convincing. As Dos Passos's passionate social conscience, with *U.S.A.*'s endeavor to grasp a whole society through its written language, made him a world figure, his technical influence starting with the French led by Sartre to Günter Grass, Norman Mailer, the E. L. Doctorow of *Ragtime,* and the Truman Capote of *In Cold Blood,* became less fresh, or so the story goes.

The best of Dos Passos's new beginnings is in *Chosen Country* (1950), fictionalized autobiography that reworks his life and tries to account for what he's done. His most popular later book was a tribute to Katy, who becomes Lulie Harrington, "the Lady of the Lake," whose husband, the lawyer Jay Pignatelli, seems a mix of Dos and his father. The story includes Katy's relatives, genially portrayed although we are shown they could be difficult. Dos Passos romanticizes this past through his new life with Betty, Lucy, Betty's son Christopher ("Kiffy") and the continuing activity of the farm. Although his first marriage had begun in New Hampshire and at the Cape, *Chosen Country* ends with an idealized wedding trip, an epithalamion fused with the author's sense of coming home to the Virginia ground he stands on, the self-discovery achieved with Betty Holdridge. The book contains historically important sketches of Europe's First World War—the first of the wounded he saw die in combat, the deaths of a young woman he was attracted to and of her family in what he visioned as "*suicide dans l'immigration*," seen by the naive Dos Passos at first hand. It is refreshingly free of a certain meanness that his later opinions sometimes generate in his fiction.

He could not maintain the artistic and intellectual energies of his youth, had been through too much, morally as well as physically. With an old-fashioned literary education in an era when one could try to catch all life on the page, he had absorbed historical transformations from what he called Woodrow Wilson's war through the Spanish Civil War, World War II, and Stalin's takeover of Eastern Europe, but he faded out as a guide to American life (his sketches become clichés, dating quickly). In his youthful letters to Crystal and some of his memoirs Dos Passos has a warm and witty mind that, in the novelist's and journalist's work, got lost with time. Were these qualities eroded by his ambition and fervor?—or his intense rejection of bourgeois society? Would they have receded as he did the grueling work of *U.S.A.?* The novelist became a sometime polemicist and intellectual hero of the Right, yet his later work is largely unread. On a postcard Wilson teased him about a piece in *National Review:* "Your article about Goldwater at the convention sounded like a teen-ager squealing over the Beatles."

After Hemingway's frightened suicide when he believed his brain was being damaged at the Mayo Clinic, Dos sent Crystal a message from one of the last two of their kind to the other: "Living so long is good so long as one has one's wits," he wrote. Two years later he modestly inscribed to her a re-creation of their generation's youth in *The Best Times* (1966)—"Crys: this tells about a guy you used to know." After an exciting visit to Easter Island in 1969 his health deteriorated. From time to time Betty and he maintained a home in Baltimore, and a small apartment served them as he went in and out of Johns Hopkins. Rheumatic fever had weakened his heart, and he died of congestive heart failure in the apartment on September 28, 1970. A memorial service followed in nearby Towson. When Crystal sent in her name on arrival, she was escorted by the usher—William F. Buckley—to a seat near Betty and Lucy.

Once Dos and Crys had delighted each other at a distance, her letters pouring out her young soul, his reflecting his integrity, authority, and wit, and backed by the novels to which he committed himself. In Spain he had said that marriage, sex, awkward as they might be, were the only thing that opened doors instead of closing them. After their trip to London they were engaged, but without a "honeymoon in Holland," and during their respective seven-month struggles apart she lost some of her glow for him. Trapped by her family situation in a Procrustean bed of a thesis, "the world's loveliest person, most delightful person" also became "its most annoying and unpredictable," as he said to Cabell Greet on Seventh Avenue. Rheumatic fever was the hand of fate, blocking their meeting in Paris after her defense. Dr. Ross cut short their New York reunion, and they proved less than courageously forthcoming with each other. A little money—and antibiotics for Dos—might have made all the difference. When her father got her back to Lockhart ("Doctor tricked me"), Crystal sank into the Texas quicksand just as she'd feared when she said that leaving Strasbourg was the "the last days of my Pompeii."

She subscribed to a wife and mother's commitments, holding onto the threads of the present, curious, she said, to know "how it all turns out." Resilient and spirited, attuned to people and situations, in correspondence and conversation she remained the presence of her letters, enlarging lives from local acquaintances to the Supreme Court justice who inscribed a book to this "great refugee from Texas." She was politically liberal and, like other women of the educated class, "canceled out Lewis's vote," as she put it with a smile, supporting Stevenson and Robert Kennedy over Lyndon Johnson, although her papers contain a letter from Lady Bird admiring her literary style.

When Townsend Ludington realized her place in the novelist's life and got in touch with her, she outlined their story, and upon finishing told him she was happy with the life she had chosen. She would have been glad to have had two lives and spent one with Lewis, the other with John Dos Passos—but, on the train from Paris to Strasbourg in 1923, she had told herself that "I'll live but once." She wrote to thank Ludington for a copy of the biography, published when she was eighty:

Dear dear Townsend Ludington,

This is a good true valuable biography—for me treasure immeasurable. Thank you for your remarkable achievement and thank you for my "compliments of the author."

My vision has deteriorated sharply. Two branch-vein occlusions. Laser has not helped. I can read guardedly with strong aids. No pain, no self pity, considerable self-indulgence. As Dos remarked [in the note to her after Hemingway shot himself], "Living so long is good as long as one keeps one's wits." I hope your life rounds out in health, happiness, joyful longevity.

Cheers, luck, affection, esteem.

Crystal Ross Dabney February 16 [1981]

On her "maiden voyage" on the *Rochambeau* she had written: "I want to be a seagull and sleep on a cresting wave. I am a seagull, but I'm not sleepy yet." Crystal died, wits sharp as ever, May 16, 1995, six weeks shy of her ninety-fifth birthday. Once she had written of Dos, "It is important to me that I'm important to him, because when once you have thought of anyone in one way, a way in which one can think of very few people in the world, one cannot be free of closeness to that person." He had the same view. They were extraordinary people and, though neither was a risk-taker in human relations, they maintained their allegiance and loyalty. The bond never broke. In Crystal's bureau drawer, along with the letters, was the large emerald ring Dos gave her in 1924, which after her death she wanted returned to Lucy for his grandson John Dos Passos Coggin. When the drawer was opened, the ring had vanished. The letters remain.

APPENDIX A
ERNEST HEMINGWAY, EXPATRIATE

Crystal Ross [Dabney]

Review of *The Sun Also Rises, Dallas News,* January 1927

Ernest Hemingway anticipates and cripples his critics in this dialogue between Jacob Barnes, the protagonist of "The Sun Also Rises," and his friend, Bill Gorton, at breakfast in the little inn of Burguete, (Northern Pyrenees), where they are spending the cold nights between hot sunny days of trout fishing, waiting for the fiesta to explode at Pamplona, up on the plateau:

"Aw, hell!" I said. "It's too early in the morning."

"There you go! And you claim to be 'a writer,' too. You're only a newspaper man—an expatriated newspaper man. You ought to be ironical. The minute you get out of bed. You ought to wake up with your mouth full of pity."

"Go on," I said. "Who did you get this stuff from?"

"Everybody. Don't you read? Don't you ever see anybody? You know what you are. You're an expatriate. Why don't you live in New York? Then you'd know these things. What do you want me to do? Come over here and tell you every year?"

"Take some more coffee," I said.

"Good! Coffee is good for you. It's the caffeine in it. Caffeine, we are here. You know what's the trouble with you? You're an expatriate. One of the worst type. Haven't you ever heard that? Nobody that ever left their own country ever wrote anything worth printing, not even in the newspapers."

He drank his coffee.

"You're an expatriate. You've lost touch with the soil. You get precious. Fake European standards have ruined you. You drink yourself to death. You become obsessed by sex. You spend all your time talking, not working. You are an expatriate. See? You hang around cafes."

"It sounds like a swell life," I said. "When do I work?"

"You don't work."

Curiously, perhaps deliberately, this humorous sprint in dialogue might be aimed at the author himself. For Hemingway does live in Paris; he does sit around cafes. One sees him almost daily, at the Rotonde, the Donue, the Select, and he and his wife, Hadley, visit regularly the bal musette near the Pantheon, which Ford Madox Ford reserves on Fridays for American and English literary exiles. I first met the Hemingways, by arrangement of mutual friends, on the terrace at the Closerie des Lilas, where Jake Barnes drank Pernod, commenting thus:

"Pernod is greenish imitation absinthe. When you add water, it turns milky. It tastes like licorice and it has a good uplift, but it drops you just as far."

After an aperitif, we dined at Lavingne's and went to a wrestling match. The Hemingways are sport enthusiasts. They participate as well as watch. He is an amateur middle-weight boxing champion, and she observes with accurate enthusiasm "short jabs and infighting," and plays tennis with interesting skill. At this time (late in June, 1924) they were preparing for their summer excursion into Spain, to the fiesta at Pamplona. (A similar excursion forms in part the theme and setting of "The Sun Also Rises.") Responding to their enthusiasm, I "went along." A party of nine, we left Paris for Bayonne, then went to St. Jean de Pied du Port, and walked from here over the Pass of Roland to Burguette (where the fishing is good), and on through the mountains, by Aolz and into Pamplona on schedule for the fiesta. This circumstance indicates the unusual interest the book has for me, and at the same time, perhaps, vitiates my ability to criticize it.

Ernest Hemingway chooses, he says, to live in Paris for three reasons: It is cheaper to live there; one gets from there a change in scene and environment impossible in America—at small expense; he likes a bit of wine with his meals. His wife adds, "But we still have to take the boy home to see America." Hemingway dislikes being called a literary exile. He is not precious nor esoteric, nor against America, nor disgruntled, nor neurotic, nor, as he says, a "talker on art." He went to the war from the Middle West and remained abroad in France and Spain and Italy as a newspaper correspondent, and now he has settled in Paris on the Rue Notre Dame des Champs with a sawmill in his front yard, a block from the crossing of the Boulevard Raspail and the Boulevard Montparnasse, where Bohemian life scintillates—and festers. Robust, hulking, handsome, vivid, he is probably the slouchiest figure in Montmartre. Throughout the seasons he wears canvas shoes; in summer, tennis trousers and sport shirts; in winter, tweeds and brown flannel blouses; almost always a Basque beret. This fashion of dress is not an affectation; it is a naturalism.

"The Sun Also Rises," impatiently awaited as the first full-length work by the author of "In Our Time," a group of short stories—this eventual first novel, published in October, was heralded at once as a novelty. Among certain groups the book has become fashionable, as a new color in crepe de chine, or a chewing gum of a new shape or unfamiliar flavor. A Princeton man, native to New York City, returning from exile in Texas, asked his brother, a Harvard man, both of them well along the alphabet of careful education, what new books he should read. "The Sun Also Rises" is the answer. "And what else?" he queried. "There are no others books," he was told.

By this very token, to others of a more pattern-cut generation, the book is unintelligible, or uninteresting, perhaps irritating. It tells of a group of Americans and English variously lost or accidentally anchored in Europe, tells of their drifting about Paris and drinking, of their drifting down into Spain to drink and to fish, to drink and to look about the annual fiesta at Pamplona with its week of bullfights. Only three of the characters, not one of whom, I venture, is entirely the product of the author's imagination, are intrinsically interesting: Jake and Lady Ashley and Bill. Jake is the aimless narrator. The supreme triumph of the book is of style over matter. For through the power of their presentation these unimportant people and their futilities are not only actual—they are absorbing. This is the greatest tribute to the author's style—that the almost painful tension is never broken—yet there is no story. The book closes in dialogue between Brett (Lady Ashley), who has just sent away an ingenuous 19-year-old matador, resolving she will henceforth continue her adventures to men of her own age, and Jake, a hopeless and tragic invalid. Recognizing that life will not permit them the consummation of their love, they make other plans and go out to drink and talk and see Madrid.

> "Oh, Jake." Brett said, "we could have had such a damned good
> time together." Ahead was a mounted policeman in khaki directing
> traffic. He raised his baton. The car slowed suddenly pressing Brett
> against me.
> "Yes," I said. "Isn't it pretty to think so?"

Here, I think, lies the crux of the criticism, the great divide of opinion: There is the old hue and cry of "Why write about it, even if it is? Why waste artistic integrity on people who don't matter?" And the counter exclamations: "Let a man dare to feel and express directly the life about and in him, whatever it is. Is a book to be excluded because it is a novel and 'unliterary,' although it is actual?" The truth, here more than usually, lies between. To say it quickly, Ernest Hemingway's style is remarkable and exciting, and his book is valuable; it is not so valuable as his style.

The story has more edge than meaning. That is perhaps the author's deliberate intention. He has made no attempt to interpret or even to challenge his material. There it is, a carbon copy of a not very significant surface of life in Paris. He reports vividly, correctly, the endless vapid talk and indolent thinking of characters more trivial than the wine glasses wherein they seek and obliterate their daily emotions. The things he writes about seem scarcely worth the care of his artistic energy. But what of it? The thing is perfectly done.

To explain the brilliant hardness of this book, its vivid sustained tension, one needs to study its style—a prose style, purest American, a mode nearer the conventions of speech than of books, a style with no affected naivete—it is natural, vigorous, alive, direct. Hemingway says things after the ways of the average vocabulary of young people about the world, but with superb economy, not a wasted word, not a padded nuance.

Has he learned of Sherwood Anderson and Ring Lardner the use of the American idiom? Perhaps, but he writes like neither. All he has learned from them is a respect for the American vernacular and confidence in his handling of it. His stye is as the textbooks have it, his own. Terse, precise, this prose is almost aggressively fresh and it includes, I think, some of the finest dialogue in existence:

"You're cock-eyed," I said.
"On wine?"
"Why not?"
"It's the humidity," Bill said.
"They ought to take this damned humidity away."

"Have another shot."

"Is this all we've got?"

"Only the two bottles."

"Do you know what you are?"

Bill looked at the bottle affectionately.

"No," I said.

"You're in the pay of the Anti-Saloon League."

"Well," I said, "the saloon must go."

"You're right there, old classmate," said Bill. "The saloon must go, and I will take it with me."

The sentences are short, abrupt, lean, statements of fact. He recites petty, unimportant details to the verge of boring, but his method justifies itself, for by the very precision and profuseness of his details he achieves an eventual economy. Saying one thing implies another. The atmosphere implies more than the individual parts. There is a cumulative richness, unsuspected subtleties of mood and emotion arrived at, not through analysis and explanations, but because their essential qualities are there. He writes essentials. His pronounced gift is seizing the essential qualities with an astonishing absoluteness, of grasping precise details and lending them meaning and individuality. It is, then, a crisp, terse, staccato style, which consists largely of setting down innumerable details left to be blended in the reader's mind, so that by his superb reporting—as a journalist, not a spy—in the rhythms of American speech, he fuses the soggy, disjointed complexity of a few bewildered lives into the fluid of creation. These self-styled "rotters" are not sentimental. Nor is their author. There is sweetness and gayiety and courage and numb endurances about these, in literary terminology, "disillusioned expatriates," but that is the sort of thing this book emanates, but does not consciously include. Jake may be impotent to live; his mind remains muscular. The author lends to his characters the cool restraint of his own style. As there is no fine writing, there is no sentimentality. Every item, every word seems to have been weighed and polished before it was included. Hemingway carries the objective method to the utmost limit. In "In Our Time" he heightens by this method the intensity and significance of each story. In "The Sun Also Rises," with the extreme indifference of a Maupassant, he simply presents a story, vivid of itself, not of his vision. The short stories are hard to the point of cruelty; they are terrible and beautiful.

This novel is neither; it is forthright, actual and fine. It has the unbounded vigor and the crisp accuracy of the stories, but not the enthusiasm that, repressed and controlled, characterized them. In "In Our Time" the irony is tangible. The novel does not need to be ironical; Jake "sits tight" and the idiocy of all in sight is apparent.

The novel has descriptive flourishes that the stories do not indulge. One notable feature is its description of the "corrida." Ernest Hemingway understands, perhaps better than any foreigner ever has, Spanish bullfighting. He has experienced it to understand it. He is aficionado; that is, he likes bullfighting for its own sake, not as a fad or a profession. He has managed to convey something what Havelock Ellis calls "The Soul of Spain," that is, the peculiar heroic energy of her spirit, into his description of the fights, and the whole mosaic of her, the stoicism, the ritualism, the intolerance, the passion, the mysticism, the art, the laziness and the pride are conveyed but never mentioned or even implied, in his record of the facts of the fiesta. This is noteworthy:

During Romero's first bull his hurt face had been very noticeable. Everything he did showed it. All the concentration of the awkwardly delicate working with the bull that could not see well brought it out. The fight had not touched his spirit, but his face had been smashed and his body hurt. He was wiping all that out now. Each thing that he did with this bull wiped that out a little cleaner. It was a good bull, a big bull and with horns, and it turned and recharged easily and surely. He was what Romero wanted in bulls.

The bull was squared on all four feet to be killed, and Romero killed directly below us. He killed, not as he had been forced to by the last bull, but as he wanted to. He profiled directly in front of the bull, drew the sword out of the folds of the muleta and sighted along the blade. The bull watched him. Romero spoke to the bull and tapped one of his feet. The bull charged and Romero waited for the charge, the muleta held low, sighting along the blade, his feet firm. Then, without taking a step forward, he became one with the bull, the sword was in high between the shoulders, the bull had followed the low-swung flannel that disappeared as Romero lurched clear to the left and it was over. The bull tried to go forward. His legs commenced to settle, he swung from side to side, hesitated, then went down on his knees—and the bull went over twitching and rigid.

In conclusion—one concludes to pretend dignity and imply unity—Mr. Hemingway's critics may question the importance of his terms, but not the energy and the honest beauty of the execution; his friends and those of his own generation in the reading public, identifying themselves in the speech and mannerisms of his characters, rejoice in the vicarious expression his art permits them.

APPENDIX B
ERNEST HEMINGWAY'S SHORT STORIES
ARE PATTERNS OF STARK SIMPLICITY

MEN WITHOUT WOMEN CHARACTERIZED
BY PIERCING TRUTH AND SANITY

Crystal Ross Dabney

Dallas News, November 6, 1927

"Men without Women," Hemingway calls his group of thirteen short stories published this October by Charles Scribner's Sons. Here is a book to make folks fling up their new fall hats and forget them, while the critics exclaim. For that instantly acclaimed author of *The Sun Also Rises* is here at his best.

This amazing young American excels in the "petit genre" which dominates, in these United States, all other literary forms. Granted that the preponderance of American short stories are sloppily written trash. Boileau has said that a single sonnet without fault is alone worth a long poem. Then how refreshing it is to read these stories of supple originality, prepared and presented with technical care, as jewels are cut and polished.

The stories in the book are incident to bullfighting in Spain, to prize-fighting in New Jersey, to convalescing in a military hospital in Italy, to adolescing in Canada, to skiing in Austria, to the contemplated murder of a Swede in a lunchroom in the town of Summit, to the drugging of

Mr. William Campbell's d.t.s in Kansas City, to the conversation of three Roman soldiers in a tavern on the evening of the crucifixion of Christ and in the trailing about Europe of strays, serious and gay, in weary after-the-war precocity.

Master of Colloquial Art

The originality, the fidelity, the dramatic vigor, the studied-to-perfect simplicity of these stories prove Hemingway's astounding power as a writer in our time, and in all those times when people shall be sensitive to colloquial art. For in his writing, the emotional and the intellectual join in a curious colloquial union; and in this union, those elements we called intellectual betray a subtle technical skill, and what we called emotion reveals a delicate forever-half-hidden spirituality; and this, through Hemingway's medium of stripped prose, is startling.

Unlike Guy de Maupassant, Hemingway has no impulse to stand between his reader and his creation—his written observation—and suggest or imply. Unlike D. H. Lawrence, he sets himself no psycho-analytic office, impolitely to rifle into the souls of a people, or a landscape or a dog, in semi-mystic jargon. Hemingway's language is geared down, lucid, conductive. His thinking is hard and clear; it does not swerve into, nor from, its own irony.

Excludes Nonessentials

The style is the man, textbooks say. So being, how proud and deliberate and stark, a Hemingway. His sentences are pared to the essential bone, enunciating thus the marrow. This author has an uncommon power of revealing the emotion behind a single word or action—an uncommon power to choose or to invent that word or that action that will betray the turbulence of the truth underneath—and an uncommon delicacy in omitting detail, or in chipping off edges without marring contours or content.

This hardness and clarity of his mind makes sharp distinctions; he expresses them, however, with singular sobriety so that we are reminded of translucent geometrical screens in black frames, or white or gray, through which we observe brilliant colors just beginning to fade (for Hemingway seems to feel that illusion does not persist, that presently the bravest sail spills its wind).

This manner of writing is conscious, studied to the least comma. It is as if the photographer were very tightly holding together a particularly small camera, as he takes his picture. Such specialized writing must strain the reader until he acquires faith in its comprehensive clarity. Perhaps for only two groups of readers would there be no initial strain—for those sophisticates who are familiar with Hemingway's idiom and adaptable to each separate ambiency, and to that careless or greater division of non-reading men to whom conglomerate methods are distasteful but who give to skillful simplicity instantaneous recognition. The In-betweeners must perhaps serve an apprenticeship of persistence to understand what is to them a singular approach to a devastating point of view.

Nor are these stories of equal interest or value. Their subjects are too diverse and their interest only average, too narrow for their appeal to be "universal." But each of them has vitality or authenticity or both, and their astonishing disparity enriches any reader.

A "Superb" Reporter

Reviewers are in the habit of saying that this or that realist is a "superb reporter." They have said this of Hemingway. But if this label is applied to John Dos Passos with his uncanny perceiving and recording of detail, his use of all his faculties as reporting functions, it is not true of Hemingway. Nor is he objective in that way Flaubert sought to teach Maupassant, that he might look at any tree until that tree was different from all others and then explain this difference. Critics need to distinguish "superb reporters" and to define "objective" and other of their worn terms under the sun. For Hemingway is objective in that he is dispassionate; he is even objective in the first person. And he is this kind of superb reporter: His exterior experience of life has been uncommonly varied and interesting and through an inner process, call it mental, emotional, artistic, he has boiled down certain of his experiences and observations and presented them through a deliberate art, so perfected as to seem an eighth wisdom, adapted to whosoever will.

Six of these thirteen stories will stand easily in art and interest alongside six of the classic best of Maupassant's 820 stories and sketches. This is not rash praise; the reviewer has tried hard to find something derogatory to splice in here, and it comes to this: There are a lot of things written that a lot of people will like a lot better than they like Ernest Hemingway's stories.

Nor is it other than reservedly that Hemingway may be compared with Guy de Maupassant. For in the writing of this Frenchman of the celebrated reputation for impropriety, in Maupassant's stories, there are no overtones; for him the physical is not a reflection of the spiritual. He adjusts subtly, falsely, secretly, the cold mirror he holds up to his selected sections of hopeless reality. With all his reportorial lucidity he was mad and himself escaped from that cruel mirror only into the raving freedom of a strait-jacket.

Does Not Mock Emotions

But Hemingway is somehow merely true. You turn from his polite, sane mirror having glimpsed planes of bitterness and wistfulness and charm and desperation and childlike gentleness that it is given average people rarely to feel, and, feeling to recognize.

Unlike Maupassant, Hemingway does not mock those emotions by which we live and die, nor the littlest sentiment. Yet he has, too, we feel, ineluctable proofs of the eternal, universal, indestructible and omnipotent stupidity, even cupidity, of the human race. But in spite of this and in a tone incessantly detached, he shows us utter compensation for the misery he sees and knows, in the elixir of sheer sport, and in the sweetness of sheer friendship.

There are some women in this book whose title excludes them. Perhaps the author gave men that tribute, knowing that they would enjoy this book more than women, for, of the possible sexes, are not men usually most grateful for those little lean spaces of stark simplicity amidst the muddle of literature and experience?

APPENDIX C
LETTER TO THE *NEW REPUBLIC*, JULY 1939

John Dos Passos

Dear Sirs:

I did not intend to publish any account of the death of my old friend Jose Robles Pazos (the fact that he had once translated a book of mine, and well, was merely incidental; we had been friends since my first trip to Spain in 1916) until I had collected more information and possible documentary evidence from survivors of the Spanish Civil War, but the reference to him in Mr. Malcolm Cowley's reviews of my last book makes it necessary for me to request you print the following as yet incomplete outline of the events that led up to his death. As I do not possess the grounds of certitude of your reviewer and his informants, I can only offer my facts tentatively and say that to the best of my belief they are accurate.

Jose Robles was a member of a family of monarchical and generally reactionary sympathies in politics; his brother was an army officer in the entourage of Alfonso of Bourbon when he was king; one of the reasons why he preferred to live in America (he taught Spanish Literature at Johns Hopkins University in Baltimore) was his disagreement on social and political questions with his family. He was in Spain on vacation when Franco's revolt broke out, and stayed there, although he had ample opportunity to leave, because he felt it was his duty to work for the Republican cause. As he knew some Russian he was given a job in the Ministry of War and soon found himself in close contact with the Russian advisors and experts who arrived at the same time as the first shipment of munitions. He became a figure of some importance, ranked as a lieutenant colonel, although he refused to wear a uniform saying that he was a mere of civilian. In the fall of '36 friends warned him that he had made powerful enemies and had better leave the country. He decided to stay. He was arrested soon after in Valencia and held by the extralegal police under conditions of great secrecy and executed in February or March of the following year.

It must have been about the time of his death that I arrived in Spain to do some work in connection with the film *The Spanish Earth,* in which we were trying to tell the story of the civil war. His wife, whom I saw in Valencia, asked me to make inquiries to relieve her terrible uncertainty. Her idea was that as I was known to have gone to some trouble to get the cause of the Spanish Republic fairly presented in the United States, government officials would tell me frankly why Robles was being held and what the charges were against him. It might have been the same day that Liston Oak, a onetime member of the American Communist Party who held a job [in] the propaganda department in Valencia, broke the news to Jose Robles' son, Francisco Robles Villegas, a seventeen-year-old boy working as a translator in the censorship office, that his father was dead. At the same time officials were telling me that the charges against Jose Robles were not serious and that he was in no danger. Mr. Del Vayo, then foreign minister, professed ignorance and chagrin when I talked to him about the case, and promised to find out the details. The general impression that the higher-ups in Valencia tried to give was that if Robles was dead he had been kidnapped and shot by anarchist "uncontrollables." They gave the same impression to members of the U.S. Embassy staff who inquired about his fate.

It was not until I reach Madrid that I got definite information from the then chief of the republican counterespionage service that Robles had been executed by a "special section," which I gathered was under the control of the Communist Party, which took the attitude that Robles had been shot as an example to other officials because he had been overheard indiscreetly discussing military plans in a café. The "fascist spy" theory seems to be the fabrication of romantic American Communist sympathizers. I certainly did not hear it from any Spaniard.

Anybody who knew Spaniards of any stripe before the civil war will remember that they tended to carry personal independence in talk and manners to the extreme. It is only too likely that Robles, like many others who were conscious of their own sincerity of purpose, laid himself open to a frameup. For one thing, he had several interviews with his brother, who was held prisoner in Madrid, to try to induce him to join the loyalist army. My impression is that the frameup in his case was pushed to the point of execution because Russian secret agents felt that Robles knew too much about the relations between the Spanish war ministry and the Kremlin and was not, from their very special point of view, politically reliable. As always in such cases, personal enmities and social feuds probably contributed.

On my way back through Valencia, as his wife was penniless, I tried to get documentary evidence of his death from republican officials so that she could collect his American life insurance. In spite of M. Del Vayo's repeated assurances that he would have a death certificate sent here, it never appeared. Nor was it possible to get hold of any record of the indictment or trials before the "special section."

As the insurance has not yet been paid I am sure that Mr. Cowley will understand that any evidence he may have in his possession as to how Jose Robles met his death that he or his informants may have will be of great use to his wife and daughter, and I hope he will be good enough to communicate it to me. His son was captured fighting in the Republican militia in the last months of the war and, as there has been no news of him for some time, we are very much afraid that he died or was killed in one of Franco's concentration camps.

Of course this is only one story among thousands in the vast butchery that was the Spanish Civil War, but it gives us a glimpse into the bloody tangle of ruined lives that underlay the hurray for our side aspects. Understanding the personal histories of a few of the men, women and children really involved would I think free our minds somewhat from the black is black and white is white obsessions of partisanship.

Sincerely yours,
John Dos Passos

APPENDIX D
LETTER TO JOHN DOS PASSOS, 1957

Crystal Ross [Dabney]

Wednesday North wind
A brilliant morning 37°
Small craft warnings
Dry enough for manure spreading
Dear Dos,

It was a delight to see you. I cherish the idea of knowing your family and vice versa. Than longen folk—there will be opportunity for pilgrimage. Love to Betty and your young.

Holy Week was a honey here. Easter, a blitz. Seventeen at table. Eggs hidden and hunted between showers. Dear good little children bored, chastened, numerous. Ross in sickening pain having been the night before in his cheerful role as a favorite horse in the concerted assault of four rowdy riders—an old football muscle—it takes time. Adult egos crescendoed in loud argument—asseveration and reasseverations. Enfin, equity and wit prevailed—maps, chess, books, records. Two guest cars slithered into approaching ditches (not *our* ditches); a third settled into trouble in the turf (ours). In the confusion of arranging dormitories I had obscured Mr. Dabney's town clothes. We had a deadline to meet.

Lewis considered with customary fatalism that Thurman had taken them by mistake. The search so aged me that there was little relief in success.

Now I am heady with tranquility—solitude and silence. The weather is still raw—seasonal projects retarded. I am glad of an interval for reconnaissance and to savour—I forgot to show you the Murphy beds for scions in the Reading Room. They're good-and-long, behind the panel in the bookshelves—a feat.

What I meant about remembering for our children their childhood was not to regale and rejoice with legend and tradition but to try to illumine some of the sources of their violence, bias, insecurity, taste and distaste, rabbit-thumping to the purpose of adult self orientation and, or, of expiating parental liabilities of com and omission. The idea was likely just a device to feel important to them and even now seems irrelevant—unless there is time for cabbages and kings and to walk with oysters on the sand.

I enclose a spare carbon for continuity and will not circularize you further. Doctor, my father, kept his progeny written to as a group for forty years. I wrote to him sometimes as inclusively but usually to him—and—scions. He lived alone (with Mexican help). These current tinkling epistles are addressed to my brothers and sisters, copies to scions interlarded with "personals." They are never acknowledged, perhaps not read. My younger brother Raleigh relishes our news I think. He is tops as a person, grimly overworked being a grimly conscientious surgeon (chest etc.) himself crippled since Saipan. He lives in Austin. Doctor was a pipeline for home truths, county and state spoon river items which he digested and relayed with stern independence. His matter of course was medical. Not wanting him to disappear entirely immediately upon demise I have assumed some of his routines. That however is not the way—my communications becoming merely salutations and a diarrhea of Dabney doings. Perhaps I can let him speak for himself now and then from his files I have here. To the post—à bientôt. Love and luck, Crys.

—Glad I didn't make the mailbox. Must tell you this has been a celestial day—land, water, sky—winter cleansed but spring—hundreds of geese here, and a few swan—one feeds ashore—hurt I think. With Olympian efficacy I have moved two fences (one, barbed wire) reseated the black raspberries, achieved a compact asparagus bed, wrested honeysuckle from Squire's rose fence, tractored tons winter felled tree trunks down to the bank rolling them over onto prepared nets of brush, reset the bell pole, cemented ominous in two major trees, whitewashed several dependencies, rearranged box, spread loads and loads of manure with exhilarating extravagance—you will know how simple and how rewarding these reforms and remedies are in the *very* early spring.

L & L, C. R. D.
Some muscles party to me are mortal sore. They say companionably: Let it rain tomorrow; let it pour.

INDEX